The Simple Guide to SAS®:
From Null to Novice

Kirby Thomas

sas.com/books

Contents

About The Author

 **Kirby Thomas** is a Technical Communicator at SAS who enjoys taking complex concepts and breaking them down into easy-to-understand steps. She has a PhD in Sociology from Florida State University, where her research focused on why women are less likely than men to major and persist in science, technology, engineering, and mathematics (STEM) fields. Her passion for creating more accessible and equitable learning environments was cultivated in her job at the Florida Department of Education and continues to motivate her work every day. She has over 9 years of experience programming in SAS and is excited to share her lessons learned with new programmers so that they can feel empowered to dive into coding without the hindrance of perfection paralysis.

Learn more about this author by visiting her author page at https://support.sas.com/en/books/authors/kirby-thomas.html. There you can download free book excerpts, access example code and data, read the latest reviews, get updates, and more.

Acknowledgments

First and foremost, thank you to Megan Jones. Without you, this book would not exist. Your encouragement, faith in me, and eagerness to learn inspired me and will undoubtedly inspire so many others.

Greg Hand, thank you for sharing your screen and allowing me to watch you code in SAS for hours while I learned. You had unending patience for all of my questions and genuinely wanted me to succeed. Without your gentle nudging, I would still be getting lost in DO loops and avoiding macros, and my code would suffer for it.

To my amazing family, your support, guidance, feedback, and time are appreciated more than you know. From brainstorming book titles and providing design advice to taking chores and errands off of my to-do list, I have never felt alone in this endeavor. I am so grateful for each one of you every single day.

Finally, thank you to all of the people who helped review, edit, format, and prepare this book for publication. Each person who touched this book made it better. Special thanks to Catherine Connolly, Suzanne Morgen, Paul Grant, Kim Lewis, Kathryn McLawhorn, Melissa Sandahl, Kyle Thomas, Robert Harris, and Mandy Byrdic. If you find this book useful, it is because of them.

Part One: Getting Started with SAS

1 Introduction

1.1 Note of Encouragement

There is a common misconception that you must know everything there is to know about coding before you begin and that there is no room for errors. This could not be further from the truth. The best way to learn how to code is simply to start coding and to make a ton of mistakes along the way. There are ways to minimize the risk of these mistakes (like making specific data sets Read-Only) and ways to avoid common errors altogether by learning from the misfortune of others (my pain is your gain). Coding is messy, frustrating, and nonlinear, but there is nothing quite like the feeling of accomplishment after struggling with a program and ending up with your desired results.

1.2 Purpose of this Guide

When I started programming in SAS, I struggled to find the best resource to help me learn. User Manuals were dense and hard to read. Videos were helpful but did not provide syntax and explanations I could refer back to. I relied heavily on Google, but it always took time to find the right article or blog post, and I would have to find that web page again the next time I needed to use that code or function. I cataloged my journey through various scattered web bookmarks and an unformatted, ever-growing Word document saved to my desktop with random code snippets and explanations. As I continued my coding journey, I relied heavily on this haphazard reference guide I had created, often searching for keywords to find the piece of code I needed.

I programmed like this for 8 years before a friend reached out to me for some tips on how to start coding with SAS. I opened my makeshift guide, and, as I stared bewildered at the unorganized wall of text, I realized that it was completely unhelpful to anyone but me. I decided that the best path forward was to do a complete overhaul of my document, organizing the information by topic, explaining common business problems and how to solve them using SAS, detailing common pitfalls to avoid, and providing example code. The document became the story of my SAS journey, which is still close to the beginning, and all the struggles and pitfalls I have encountered along the way. The result was this guide, which is intended to help new coders learn the basics and get started with using SAS.

This guide is meant to be a living, breathing document that grows with you along your SAS journey. Please add your own thoughts, experiences, and code examples that are most relevant to your work to the companion template that can be downloaded at https://support.sas.com/en/books/authors/kirby-thomas.html. You can also reinforce your learning by viewing helpful video tutorials at https://video.sas.com/, find a training course (sas.com/training), or check out a local SAS User Group (https://www.sas.com/en_us/connect/user-groups.html). It is my sincerest hope that you build upon the information in this guide with your own knowledge and experiences so that it far surpasses the usefulness that it holds in its original form. Let's jump in!

2 Getting Started

The field of data analytics is fast-paced, ever-evolving, and often intimidating to newcomers, but learning how to leverage data analytics is a critical skill that can enrich your life in so many ways. Not only can it dramatically increase your marketability and financial security, as many companies compete to hire and retain talent in these positions, but your work can lead to real policy changes that can positively impact the world. For example, data analytics has been used to improve water quality, aid in natural disaster response, protect endangered species, fight human trafficking, detect fraud, track the spread of disease, and combat homelessness and food insecurity. To learn more about how analytics can help humanity, visit https://www.sas.com/en_us/data-for-good.html.

Now that we have discussed some of the benefits of data analytics, let's talk about why SAS is a great tool to help you on your learning journey. To stay competitive in the field of analytics, SAS has released a slew of products over the years to assist users with their data management, forecasting, modeling, machine learning, text analytics, and visual analytics needs, to name a few. SAS® Viya® was specifically designed as a one-stop shop software platform that allows users, businesses, and organizations to access, manage, analyze, and visualize their data all in one place. The SAS Viya® platform houses several applications like SAS® Drive to share and collaborate between users, SAS® Data Studio to prepare data, SAS® Studio to develop SAS code, SAS® Model Studio to build models, and SAS® Visual Analytics to explore and visualize data.

With all of the products SAS has to offer, it is hard to know where to start. And in my experience, starting is always the most challenging part of any new venture. Rather than trying to teach you everything there is to know about SAS, which would be overwhelming and, quite frankly, outside the scope of my knowledge, my goal in creating this guide is to create a roadmap for new coders on what topics to start with to quickly learn the basics of programming in SAS. To really understand SAS and build a strong foundation, the best place to start, in my opinion, is learning Base SAS®.

Base SAS® is a programming language at the heart of all SAS Software, making it an essential step in learning SAS. Base SAS® is updated with new functionality every so often, resulting in new versions. I am using SAS 9.4 (maintenance release TS1M7) for all examples in this guide, so minor modifications might be required if you are working in a different version. SAS® Studio (web-based), SAS® Enterprise Guide® (Windows client application), and the SAS Windowing Environment (locally installed) are all Graphical User Interfaces (GUIs) that can be used to develop and run Base SAS® code. Most of the code discussed in this guide will work on any of these interfaces, and although each GUI operates a little differently, Base SAS® is the common language used for all of them.

2.1 SAS Windows

There are four universal components to know about when getting started, no matter which SAS programming GUI you use: the Editor window, Log window, Output Data window, and Results window. They usually appear as tabs (Code, Log, Output Data, and Results) under each SAS program, and you can customize the layout of these windows in many ways. Try out different layout views and find what works best for you.

1. The **Editor window** (Code tab) in Figure 1 is where you do most of your coding. This is where you enter and save the syntax— or properly structured code— for your program. There are line numbers on the left-hand side of the window for easy reference. You can run entire programs or highlight a few lines of code within a program and only run the portion of code that you selected. This is helpful when you are building a new program or troubleshooting a bug in your code. You might want to run one step at a time and view your results. Be sure to *save your programs often* as you work so that you don't lose work if your computer dies, restarts unexpectedly, you time out, or get kicked off of your online session. Every data analyst has at least one horror story about losing several hours of code work because they didn't save — or at least that's what I tell myself to sleep better at night.

Figure 1: Editor Window

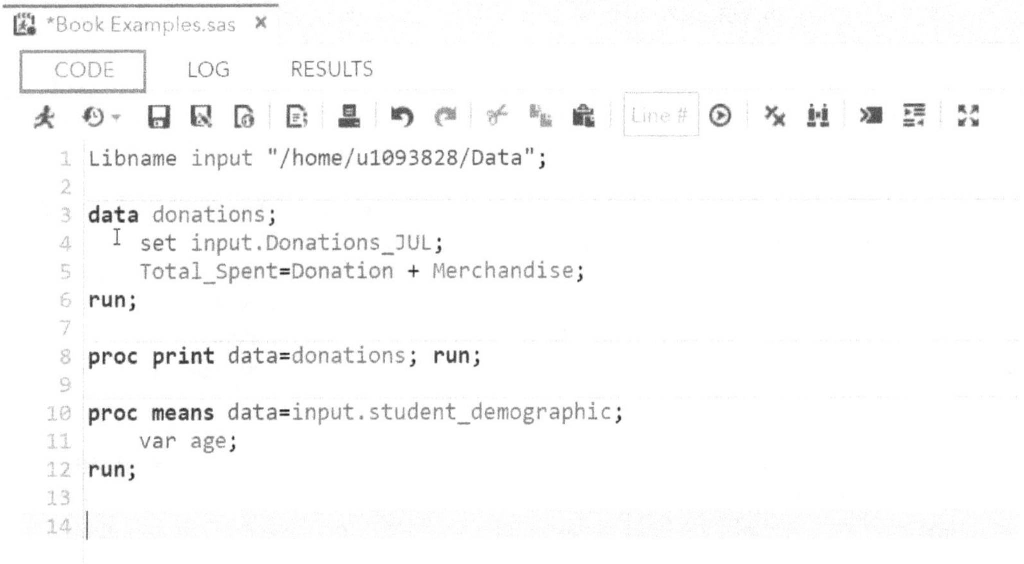

```
    *Book Examples.sas   ✕

    CODE        LOG      RESULTS

  1  Libname input "/home/u1093828/Data";
  2
  3  data donations;
  4    I set input.Donations_JUL;
  5        Total_Spent=Donation + Merchandise;
  6  run;
  7
  8  proc print data=donations; run;
  9
 10  proc means data=input.student_demographic;
 11      var age;
 12  run;
 13
 14  |
```

2. The **Log window,** displayed in Figure 2, provides information about how your code ran. It lists notes during program execution, warnings, and error messages if encountered. If there is an error in your code, a message will appear in red in the

log under the statement that caused the error. Notes appear in blue, and warning messages in green. Use the log messages to help you troubleshoot any issues you encounter when executing your code. ***Always check the log*** after running any code to ensure it ran the way you expected it to. The log also provides additional useful information like the number of variables and observations in each data set and how long it took to process each DATA step. This can be invaluable information for you if you need to know which part of the code was taking the longest to run. There are statements and options that allow users to customize their logs by adjusting the appearance of the log, suppressing certain contents of the log, or writing additional information to the log. More information about these statements and options can be found at: https://go.documentation.sas.com/doc/en/pgmsascdc/9.4_3.5/lepg/p119kau8rt2ebgn1bzaipafu6jp3.htm.

Figure 2: Log Window

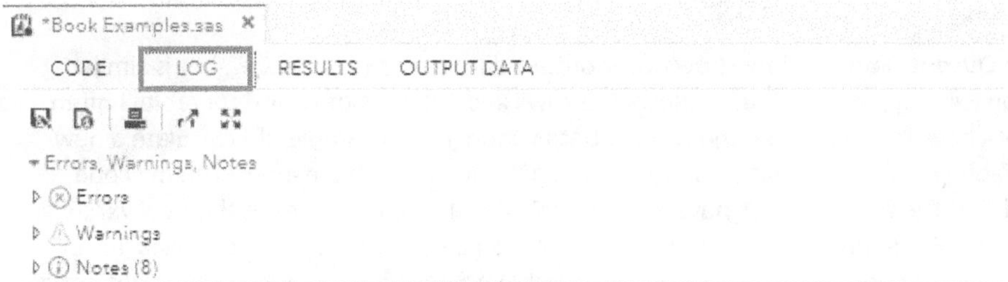

```
                 *Book Examples.sas  ✕

        CODE        LOG       RESULTS     OUTPUT DATA

       ⊠  ⊡   |  ⊒  ⋔  ⛶

     ▾ Errors, Warnings, Notes
     ▷ ⊗ Errors
     ▷ ⚠ Warnings
     ▷ ⓘ Notes (8)

        1          OPTIONS NONOTES NOSTIMER NOSOURCE NOSYNTAXCHECK;
        68
        69         Libname input "/home/u1093828/Data";
     NOTE: Libref INPUT was successfully assigned as follows:
             Engine:         V9
             Physical Name: /home/u1093828/Data
        70
        71         data donations;
        72         set input.Donations_JUL;
        73         Total_Spent=Donation + Merchandise;
        74         run;

     NOTE: There were 3 observations read from the data set INPUT.DONATIONS_JUL.
     NOTE: The data set WORK.DONATIONS has 3 observations and 8 variables.
     NOTE: DATA statement used (Total process time):
             real time             0.00 seconds
             user cpu time         0.00 seconds
             system cpu time       0.00 seconds
             memory                950.03k
             OS Memory             21160.00k
             Timestamp             09/19/2023 08:02:06 PM
             Step Count                      35  Switch Count  2
             Page Faults                     1
             Page Reclaims                   203
             Page Swaps                      0
             Voluntary Context Switches      24
             Involuntary Context Switches    0
             Block Input Operations          480
             Block Output Operations         264
```

```
75
76          proc print data=donations; run;

NOTE: There were 3 observations read from the data set WORK.DONATIONS.
NOTE: PROCEDURE PRINT used (Total process time):
      real time            0.01 seconds
      user cpu time        0.01 seconds
      system cpu time      0.00 seconds
      memory               1246.59k
      OS Memory            21156.00k
      Timestamp            09/19/2023 08:02:06 PM
      Step Count                       36  Switch Count   0
      Page Faults                      0
      Page Reclaims                    180
      Page Swaps                       0
      Voluntary Context Switches       0
      Involuntary Context Switches     0
      Block Input Operations           0
```

3. The **Output Data window** shows your output data tables (see Figure 3). It is similar to an Excel spreadsheet, as it shows the rows and columns of your data table. I often spot-check my code using the Output Data window. For example, if I calculate a new variable, I make sure that variable shows up in my output table after I run my code and that the first few rows have the appropriate calculated values in the new variable column. Remember, SAS will not always give you an error if you make a mistake. For example, suppose you type the wrong variable name in a calculation. SAS might not give you an error in the log because the wrong variable does exist in your data. However, the calculation itself is wrong because you meant to use a different variable. The most important lesson about programming in SAS (and programming in general) is that programs run exactly what you type/tell them to run, ***not what you meant to run***. So always spot-check your output for accuracy.

Figure 3: Output Data Window

4. Finally, the **Results window** in Figure 4 displays any written output such as descriptions, calculations from SAS procedures, or sample data. Throughout this guide, the word

print is used to indicate outputting information to the results window. For example, suppose you would like to see a data table description. You can run PROC CONTENTS on this table, and the results of this procedure are printed to the Results window for you to view. If you want to know the mean value of one of the variables in your data set, you can run PROC MEANS on the variable and view the results in this window. It takes SAS time to print results for you, so avoid printing large data sets (PROC PRINT) or frequencies (PROC FREQ) for variables with over 100 value categories. It will take forever to run or warn you that you are trying to print out too much information to the results window. If you need to look at a large data set, it is easier to view it in your Output Data window or to export the data to Excel.

Figure 4: Results Window

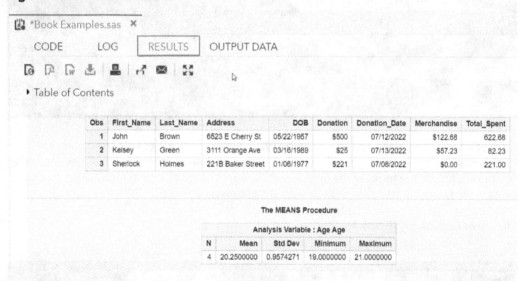

2.2 SAS® OnDemand for Academics

Now that we've covered the main components of Base SAS® GUIs, let's walk through one of these interfaces together. Since SAS® Studio is the newest of these GUIs, is offered through SAS Viya®, and is available for free on the SAS® OnDemand for Academics website, I will give a brief overview of its layout and features before diving into Base SAS® syntax.

To start using SAS® Studio for free, visit: https://welcome.oda.sas.com/. If you have not done so already, under Get Started, click **SAS Profile** to create an account (Figure 5). Fill out the required fields and click **Create Profile**.

Figure 5: SAS® OnDemand for Academics Welcome Page

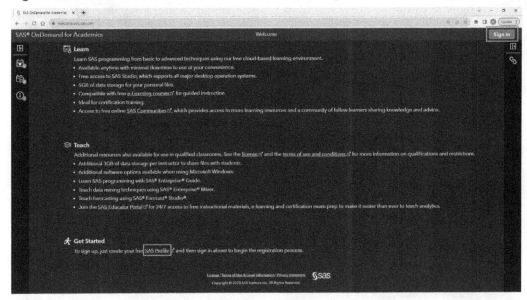

Once you have a registered account, from the Welcome page, click **Sign In** in the upper right hand corner of the screen ([Figure 5](#)) and type in your login information. Read and then check the box next to Accept the terms of the license and the terms of use and conditions. Then, click **Sign In**. Click the **Launch** button next to Code with SAS® Studio ([Figure 6](#)).

Figure 6: Launch SAS® Studio

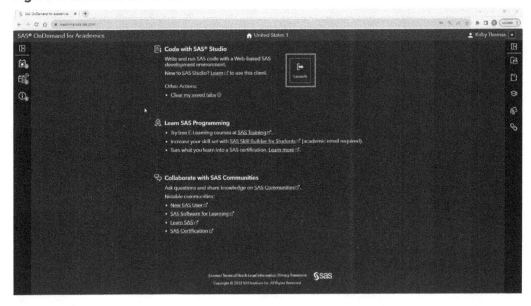

SAS® Studio opens in a new tab in your browser.

2.3 SAS® Studio

SAS® Studio is a web-based programming interface that connects to a local or hosted SAS server. When you log on, a new session initiates, and a navigation pane appears on the left side of the screen while a work area appears on the right side. You might see a Start Page in the work area where you can select **New SAS Program**, or SAS® Studio might have already opened a new program for you. By default, a new Program tab reads Program 1 until you save it (Figure 7).

Figure 7: Screenshot of a New SAS Program in SAS® Studio

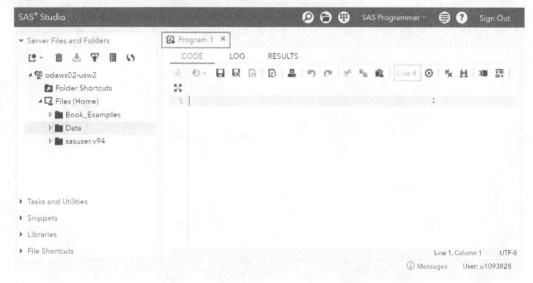

Once saved, the Program tab will display the program name that you chose. SAS programs are saved with the .sas file extension and SAS tables are saved with the .sas7bdat file extension. The Program tab has subtabs that are discussed in detail in the SAS Windows section. At a high level, the Code subtab is where you write your SAS code, the Log displays information and errors when you run your code, the Output Data subtab displays the SAS tables that you are working with, and the Results subtab provides the results of data analysis and anything you tell SAS to print out for you. When you save your program, it saves the syntax in the Code subtab so that you can open and rerun the code later.

Note: The Output Data subtab does not appear until you read in or create a data table.

If you want SAS® Studio to automatically open the program(s) that you were working on and saved but did not close before exiting your previous SAS® Studio session (I highly recommend this), click the **hamburger icon** (three stacked lines) in the upper-right hand corner of the screen called More Application Options, then **Preferences > Start Up > Continue where you left off**[1] (Figure 8).

Figure 8: SAS Studio Preferences

The Navigation Pane is typically located on the left-hand side of the screen (Figure 7). It has five sections: Server Files and Folders, Tasks and Utilities, Snippets, Libraries, and File Shortcuts.

1. The **Server Files and Folders** section (labeled Explorer in SAS Viya®) provides access to your computer and server folders that contain files, programs, and data tables.
2. The **Tasks and Utilities** section provides a point-and-click feature that allows users to explore, visualize, and analyze data.
3. The **Snippets** section lets users save syntax that they use frequently so that they can easily paste and edit it in new programs.
4. The **Libraries** section displays the assigned SAS libraries for your session and the data tables contained in each library. You will learn more about assigning SAS libraries in the SAS Libraries section of the guide.
5. The **File Shortcuts** section enables you to create shortcuts to files on the SAS server or found at a URL and quickly access them by double-clicking or dragging the shortcut to the work area.

---

[1] In SAS® Studio V in SAS Viya®, check the bubble next to **Options > Preferences > Start Up > Restore tabs listed in Open Files pane**.

2.3.1 Tasks

While this guide focuses on writing your own code or syntax, Tasks can be a useful tool when you are unsure of the syntax needed for a procedure. You can use this point-and-click feature in SAS® Studio or SAS® Enterprise Guide® to generate the code that you need, copy the syntax, and save it to your program for future use. This syntax can then be run on any SAS GUI.

Let's walk through an example. If you want to know summary statistics about a data set but are unsure of the syntax needed to create it, click on the **Tasks** section, expand **Tasks** and then **Statistics** and double-click on **Summary Statistics** (Figure 9). A new tab called Summary Statistics opens that lets you browse and select a data table, select variables of interest, and run the generated code.

Figure 9: SAS Studio Tasks in Navigation Pane

Note: For those just getting started, SAS provides several preloaded data sets to practice with. When browsing for a data table, go to the **Libraries** section in the navigation pane, expand **My Libraries** and **SASHELP**.

In the Summary Statistics tab and Data subtab, click the **data set icon** (select a table) under Data, expand **My Libraries** and **SASHELP**, and double-click **CLASS** to load the Class table. Under Roles, click the **plus sign** over the Analysis variables box, click on **Age** and then **OK**. Next, click the **plus sign** over the Classification variables box, click on **Sex** and then **OK**. There is also an Options subtab that lets you choose which summary statistics you would like included in your output. Keep the default selections checked for now. Notice that once the required roles are filled in on the Data tab, code is generated on the right-hand side of the screen in the Code tab (Figure 10). When you click **Run** (the little running person next to the save button) or **F3** on your keyboard, the code executes, and the results are shown in the Results subtab.

Figure 10: Summary Statistics Task Generated Code

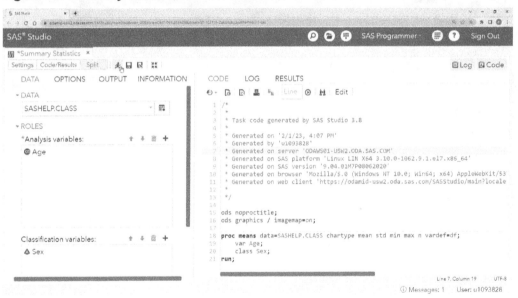

Note: The green text in the Code subtab displays comments that are not part of the SAS syntax itself but that provide helpful information about when and where the code was generated. SAS ignores comments during code execution. /* denotes the beginning of a comment, while */ denotes the end of the comment[2]. It is always good practice to include

---

[2] Pro tip: If you highlight a block of text in your code editor and then hold **Ctrl** and click **/**, SAS will comment out the entire block of text you have selected. Use this keystroke combination again to uncomment a highlighted block of code. In the SAS® Enterprise Guide®, click **Ctrl**, **Shift**, **/** to uncomment.

comments in your programs to help remind yourself or other coders that might inherit your programs of why certain decisions were made or what certain code blocks are doing.

We can see from the log that no errors occurred when running the program (Figure 11).

Figure 11: Summary Statistics Task Log

```
CODE        LOG      RESULTS

▼ Errors, Warnings, Notes
▷ ⊗ Errors
▷ ⚠ Warnings
▷ ⓘ Notes (3)

1        OPTIONS NONOTES NOSTIMER NOSOURCE NOSYNTAXCHECK;
NOTE: ODS statements in the SAS Studio environment may disable some output features.
69
70       /*
71        *
72        * Task code generated by SAS Studio 3.8
73        *
74        * Generated on '9/18/23, 5:10 PM'
75        * Generated by 'u1093828'
76        * Generated on server 'ODAWS01-USW2.ODA.SAS.COM'
77        * Generated on SAS platform 'Linux LIN X64 3.10.0-1062.9.1.el7.x86_64'
78        * Generated on SAS version '9.04.01M7P08062020'
79        * Generated on browser 'Mozilla/5.0 (Windows NT 10.0; Win64; x64) AppleWebKit/537.36 (KHTML, like Gecko)
79       ! Chrome/116.0.0.0 Safari/537.36'
80        * Generated on web client
80       ! 'https://odamid-usw2.oda.sas.com/SASStudio/main?locale=en_US&zone=GMT-04%253A00&ticket=ST-157946-0cha4ejteSF9QJzkrT5q-cas
80       ! '
81        *
82        */
83
84        ods noproctitle;
85        ods graphics / imagemap=on;
86
87        proc means data=SASHELP.CLASS chartype mean std min max n vardef=df;
88        var Age;
89        class Sex;
90        run;

NOTE: There were 19 observations read from the data set SASHELP.CLASS.
NOTE: PROCEDURE MEANS used (Total process time):
      real time              0.01 seconds
      user cpu time          0.01 seconds
      system cpu time        0.01 seconds
      memory                 9505.96k
      OS Memory              30900.00k
      Timestamp              09/18/2023 09:10:46 PM
      Step Count                        103  Switch Count  1
      Page Faults                       0
      Page Reclaims                     2109
      Page Swaps                        0
      Voluntary Context Switches        10
      Involuntary Context Switches      0
      Block Input Operations            0
      Block Output Operations           8
```

The results in Table 1 show the number of observations, the mean, standard deviation, minimum, and maximum ages for females (F) and males (M). There were 9 females in the data set with a mean age of 13.2222222, a standard deviation of 1.3944334, a minimum Age of 11, and a maximum Age of 15.

Table 1: Summary Statistics Task Results (PROC MEANS of Age by Sex)

Sex	N Obs	Mean	Std Dev	Minimum	Maximum	N
		Analysis Variable : Age				
F	9	13.2222222	1.3944334	11.0000000	15.0000000	9
M	10	13.4000000	1.6465452	11.0000000	16.0000000	10

Now you know what syntax to run the next time you need to calculate summary statistics on a data set. You can copy the code generated by the task into another program or save it to your code snippets for future use.

2.3.2 Snippets

To add the code generated in the Tasks section to your snippets, highlight the code in the **Code** subtab, **right-click** the highlighted code, and then click **Add to My Snippets**. Give your code snippet a name like Summary Statistics Task, and then click **Save**. Now you can find this code snippet by expanding **My Snippets** under the **Snippets** section of the navigation pane. When you double-click the snippet, it will paste the code into the Code subtab of the program that you are currently working in (Figure 12). You will need to edit the data set name and variable names to reflect any new data set or variables that you would like to run summary statistics on.

Figure 12: Insert Code Snippet into Program

2.4 Data Setup

The data used in this book is available for download from the SAS Author Page found at https://support.sas.com/en/books/authors/kirby-thomas.html. Once the data has been downloaded, save it to your computer. I created a folder called Book_Data on my desktop and saved the files in a subfolder called Input_Data. View the properties of the folder that you save the book data to and make note of the location. In my case, the location is: C:\Users\Kirby\ Desktop\Book_Data\Input_Data. When using SAS® Enterprise Guide® or the SAS Windowing environment, create a LIBREF called INPUT that references the location of your saved data files. In my case, I would begin my program with the following statement:

```
LIBNAME input 'C:\Users\Kirby\Desktop\Book_Data\Input_Data';
```

Update the location in single quotation marks to reflect where your data is saved.

If you are using SAS® Studio, you will need to upload the data files to the SAS server before you can work with them. First, create a folder to hold your book data. Right-click **Files** in the navigation pane and select **New > Folder**. I named my folder Data. Clever. I know. Now, right-click the folder you just created, and click **Upload Files** (Figure 13).

Figure 13: Upload Files

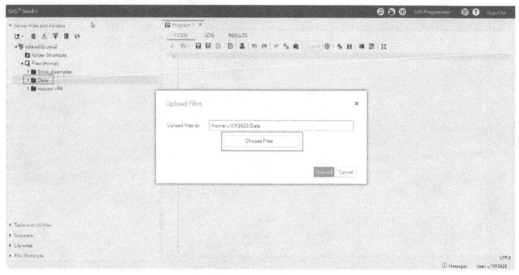

When you click **Choose Files**, the file explorer opens and enables you to navigate to where you saved your data files for this book. You can select one data file or hold down the **Ctrl** button and select several files to upload them all at once. Next, click **Open**. A list of selected files appears in the Upload Files window, and you can click the **Upload** button to upload the files to the SAS server into your Data folder.

Right-click the **Data** folder that you uploaded the files to, and then click **Properties** to copy this location. In my case, the location is: /home/u1093828/Data. Create a LIBREF called INPUT at the beginning of your SAS® Studio programs to reference any files found in this folder location:

```
LIBNAME input '/home/u1093828/Data';
```

The INPUT LIBREF will be used throughout the code examples to reference the location where the book data files are saved. More information about creating LIBNAMES can be found in the SAS Libraries section.

3 How SAS® Works

Now that you're all set up, let's dig into how SAS® works. The following definitions will be helpful to refer back to as you read through this book:

SAS data sets: Proprietary format (like Excel, Oracle, etc.). Makes data immediately available to the other elements of SAS.

PROC steps: Operate on data sets. Describe the type of procedure output (analysis, report, etc.) that you want done to a data set.

DATA steps: Process data sets on a row-by-row basis, usually to prepare the data for PROC steps.

Global statements: Used to create SAS libraries, set options, titles, footnotes, etc.

Comments: Used to document what is happening in SAS programs. SAS does not process comments.

Macro language/Macros: Enables text substitution or replacement in SAS programs.

3.1 DATA and PROC Steps

SAS syntax consists of a series of statements, and the end of each statement is denoted by a semicolon[3]. A single SAS statement can be split up onto several lines in your editor. Statements can be organized into two types of steps: the DATA step and the PROC step. While some statements can exist on their own (for example, setting up a library or certain system options), the real work in a SAS program happens within steps.

---

[3] Unless you are an avid Jane Austen reader, you have likely had little interaction with semicolons in your everyday life. Sure, they can be used to separate related independent clauses or items in a complex list, but a well-placed period or conjunction can render the semicolon virtually unnecessary. Until now. SAS programming has fully embraced the semicolon, allowing the once-overlooked punctuation mark to reign supreme. Respect the semicolon. Absorb it into your subconscious. Otherwise, you may find yourself coding early one morning before coffee, forgetting a semicolon and SET keyword, and overwriting an important data file with all null values. Theoretically, of course...

3.1.1 DATA Step

A DATA step reads in data and makes changes to it. This can include renaming or recoding variables, creating or calculating new variables, transposing data, merging data, saving it to a new location, etc. DATA steps start with the keyword DATA and end with the keyword RUN. In its most basic form, the DATA step looks like this:

```
data output-table-name(s);
        SET input-table-name(s);
run;
```

You can add a WHERE statement to the DATA step if you would like to subset your data by a certain expression, like where country is equal to "USA" or where a transaction value is over $50. You can add KEEP or DROP statements to tell SAS which variables to output in your output table. You can use a RENAME statement to change your variable names or an IF-THEN statement to apply conditional logic to your data. A MERGE statement enables you to merge two or more tables together on whatever variable(s) you specify in your BY statement. We will learn more about these statements later. Just remember that a DATA step typically changes data in some way, starts with the keyword DATA, and ends with the word RUN.

3.1.2 PROC Step

PROC steps run procedures on your data, like sorting it, calculating means, calculating frequencies, or printing certain observations. Rather than editing your data like the DATA step, PROC steps can be used to analyze and visualize your data so that you can take a deeper dive into what your data means. They start with the PROC keyword and end with the word RUN. The basic syntax for a PROC statement is:

```
proc procedure-keyword data=input-table-name;
run;
```

Procedures can also include statements like VAR and TABLES, which tell SAS which variables to include in the procedure. These statements come after the end of the PROC statement (or after the first semicolon in the PROC step). Procedures also typically have several available options that can be included to indicate how you would like the procedure to run or what calculations you would like SAS to perform and output for you. For example, you can add options for SAS to include the median and mode values of given variables in your PROC MEANS output; provide row, column, or total percentages in your frequency tables; round results; or print variable labels instead of variable names[4]. Options might be included directly in the PROC statement (or before the first semicolon) or could be included to modify the default option in a different statement in the PROC step.

---

[4] Keep reading. No subliminal messages about semicolons here.

It is easy to get overwhelmed by the number of options available when you start coding, but over time, you will start to appreciate the flexibility these options provide. You don't need to memorize these options. SAS has programming documentation that lists all of the statement types and options available for DATA steps and procedures[5]. You can bookmark helpful documentation for quick reference.

3.2 Data Structure

There are two components to SAS data sets: a descriptor portion and a data portion.

1. The **descriptor portion** contains information about the data set and the individual columns/variables in the data set. This includes information about the number of observations in the data set, the date on which it was created, whether the data is sorted, and the variable names, types, lengths, formats, informats, and labels.
2. The **data portion** of SAS data sets contains all of the variables (columns) and their values for each observation (row) in the data set. An observation is some type of entity, like a person, company, or country. It could also be a unit of time, like a day, month, or year. These entities each have attributes that can vary between observations. These attributes are called variables. For example, if you have a data set where each observation represents a person, you could have many variables associated with each person like Name, Age, Gender, Race, and Income. The information associated with each entity and variable is a value (i.e., "Mary", 39, "female", "white", $45,000). You can view the data portion of a SAS data set by looking at your Output Data tab.

3.2.1 Columns/Variables

Columns in a data set must have a name, type, and length. Column names must:

- Be between 1–32 characters
- Start with a letter or underscore
- Contain only numbers, letters, or underscores—though there are ways to get around these requirements by using the VALIDVARNAME option, which is discussed in more detail in the Importing Data section below.

Letters can be upper or lowercase, and SAS is not case-sensitive when referencing a variable name in code. Column types can be character, numeric, or date depending on the type of values in the column. Base SAS® stores data as either character or numeric data types, so dates are saved as numeric values. Column lengths should be set to the number of characters in the longest value in a character column or set to 8 for a numeric or date column.

---

[5] You can find the SAS® 9.4 And SAS Viya® 3.5 programming documentation here:
https://go.documentation.sas.com/doc/en/pgmsascdc/9.4_3.5/pgmsaswlcm/home.htm

3.2.2 Values

Case does matter when referring to data *values*[6]. Character column values can have a length up to 32,767 bytes (each character is 1 byte) and can contain letters, numbers, special characters, and blanks. A missing character value is denoted by a space (" "). Numeric column values are stored with a length of 8 bytes. They can consist of numbers, minus signs, decimal points, and E for scientific notation. SAS date values are stored as numeric values representing the number of days between January 1, 1960, and a specified date. Date values can be negative. However, most users apply date formats to these values for ease of interpretation. Missing numeric and date values are represented by a period (.).

3.2.3 PROC Contents

To view the information included in the descriptor portion of a data set, you can run PROC CONTENTS on the data set.

```
proc contents DATA=table-name;
run;
```

Table 2 shows what it looks like when I run PROC CONTENTS on one of the book data sets named Coffee.

```
proc contents data=input.coffee;
run;
```

The first box tells us that the data set name is WORK.COFFEE and that there are 9 rows/ observations in the data set and 4 variables.

The last box shows us a list of these 4 variables in alphabetic order. The variables in this data set are Afternoon_Favorites_, Division, Morning_Standard_Orders, and Name. The numbers in the first column tell us in which order these variables appear in the data set. For example, Name is the first column in the data set, followed by Division and Morning_Standard_Orders. This table also tells us that these variables are all character (stored as text), and lists the lengths, formats, informats, and labels for each variable.

---

[6] If you want to subset a data set to only the observations with a Country value of "USA", adding a WHERE statement where country="usa" *will not* pick up on any records with a country value of "USA" or "Usa" or "UsA" because *case matters* when matching to *data values*. Here, the UPCASE function can be handy (WHERE upcase(Country)="USA"). With this statement, SAS checks if the condition would be met if the values of country were all uppercase but *does not actually change the underlying values* of the variable Country. See section Calculating New Variables for information on how to create a new variable for Country with all uppercased values.

Table 2: PROC CONTENTS of Coffee Data Set

The CONTENTS Procedure

Data Set Name	INPUT.COFFEE	Observations	9
Member Type	DATA	Variables	4
Engine	V9	Indexes	0
Created	8/23/2023 10:39	Observation Length	59
Last Modified	8/23/2023 10:39	Deleted Observations	0
Protection		Compressed	NO
Data Set Type		Sorted	NO
Label			
Data Representation	SOLARIS_X86_64, LINUX_X86_64, ALPHA_TRU64, LINUX_IA64		
Encoding	utf-8 Unicode (UTF-8)		

Engine/Host Dependent Information	
Data Set Page Size	131072
Number of Data Set Pages	1
First Data Page	1
Max Obs per Page	2216
Obs in First Data Page	9
Number of Data Set Repairs	0
Filename	/home/u1093828/Data/coffee.sas7bdat
Release Created	9.0401M7
Host Created	Linux
Inode Number	17022809
Access Permission	rw-r--r--
Owner Name	u1093828
File Size	256KB
File Size (bytes)	262144

Alphabetic List of Variables and Attributes						
#	Variable	Type	Len	Format	Informat	Label
4	Afternoon_Favorites_	Char	22	$22.	$22.	Afternoon Favorites!
2	Division	Char	9	$9.	$9.	Division
3	Morning_Standard_Orders	Char	21	$21.	$21.	Morning Standard Orders
1	Name	Char	7	$7.	$7.	Name

Note: Now that we have reviewed the structure of SAS data sets, I have a few notes to keep in mind as you read through the rest of this guide. First, I use the words Variable and Column, Row and Observation, and Table and Data Set interchangeably throughout this guide. Second, because SAS is not case-sensitive when reading variable names, statements, functions, and options in code, my code is usually a mix of uppercase, lowercase, and proper case. While some of you might enjoy the Wild West of coding like I do, I understand that others find comfort in uniformity. Do what works for you.

3.3 DATA Step Processing

There are two phases in DATA step processing: compilation and execution.

1. Phase 1, **compilation**, first scans the DATA step for syntax errors. Syntax errors include things like forgotten semicolons, misspelled keywords, unmatched quotation marks or parentheses, or invalid options. If it finds any, you will get an error, and the step will stop executing and print an error message in your log. DATA steps are read character by character from top to bottom and left to right. If the code does not have any syntax errors, it is compiled into machine-executable code, and a **program data vector (PDV)**, which is an area of memory where SAS builds a data set, is created. The PDV contains all columns that will be read in or created during the DATA step, along with the assigned attributes of those variables, like whether they are character or numeric and how long they are. This is the descriptor portion of the SAS data set.
2. During the **execution** phase, the PDV holds and manipulates one row of data at a time. In this phase, SAS reads, manipulates, and writes data to one or more data sets. Errors and warnings can occur in this phase, too. For example, if the descriptor portion identified a variable as numeric, but many of the values that it reads in for that variable (as it loops through the data) are character, SAS will let you know that in the log.

In order to know where statements and options should go within a DATA step, it is essential to understand how the DATA step is processed in SAS. For example, dropping variables too soon could prevent you from doing important calculations but dropping unnecessary variables too late in the process could lead to slower processing time and performance. Let's say you need the variables Height and Weight from the Health_Chart data set (Table 3) to calculate a new variable, BMI, but you do not want the original variables in the output data set you are creating. If you drop Height and Weight too soon, the DATA step will not understand how to create BMI, and you can get errors or null (missing) values in your output data set when you run your code.

Suppose you are calculating a new variable, BMI, in a DATA step based on variables Height and Weight in the read-in (or input) data set Health_Chart, but you only want BMI (and not Health and Weight) to appear in the final data set. To do this, you can add a DROP statement to your DATA step. This ensures that Height and Weight get read into the PDV so that the BMI calculation can occur but that the Height and Weight columns get flagged and dropped when data is written to the output data set. Note that in this example, Weight is in pounds while Height is in inches.

Table 3: Health_Chart Data Set

Patient_ID	Height	Weight	Eye_Color	Age
8727172	59	118	blue	21
6015638	66	149	green	42
9242748	56	89	brown	11
1135601	63	152	brown	65
3651067	74	210	blue	34
4437097	62	100	brown	16
6417249	67	145	blue	57
9462800	60	133	brown	89
9364322	72	283	brown	38

```
data BMI;
    set input.Health_Chart;
    BMI=Weight / (Height*Height) * 703;
    drop Weight Height;
run;
```

Height and Weight are read into the PDV by the SET statement. Then the BMI variable is created and calculated. Finally, Height and Weight are dropped from the generated BMI data set before it is output.

To save space or processing time, you can drop variables that aren't needed when reading in a data set in the SET statement. That way, the column is never read into the PDV. Enclose the DROP keyword, an equal sign, and the variable name in parentheses after the SET statement to inform SAS that this variable can be completely ignored. This is called a DROP data set option rather than a DROP statement. For example, the previous Health_Chart data set has the variable, Eye_Color, that is not needed for this analysis and therefore does not need to be read in or output to the BMI data set. We should put this variable in a DROP data set option.

```
data BMI;
    set input.Health_Chart (drop=Eye_Color);
    BMI=Weight / (Height*Height) * 703;
    drop Weight Height;
run;
```

The same applies to a KEEP statement. KEEP statements provide SAS with a list of variables to include when reading in a data set (to decrease processing time) or in the output table once calculations are complete. Any variable not listed in your KEEP data set option is not read in (if it is in the SET statement). Likewise, any variable not listed in a KEEP statement or a KEEP data set option in the DATA statement is deleted at the end of the DATA step. The code below keeps the Patient_ID and BMI variables at the end of the DATA step. This code is equivalent to adding a KEEP statement to the end of the DATA step listing these two variables.

```
data BMI (keep=Patient_ID BMI);
    set input.Health_Chart;
    BMI=Weight / (Height*Height) * 703;
run;
```

Table 4: BMI Data Set

Patient_ID	BMI
8727172	23.83050847
6015638	24.04660239
9242748	19.95121173
1135601	26.92265054
3651067	26.95945946
4437097	18.28824142
6417249	22.70773001
9462800	25.97194444
9364322	38.37750772

The resulting data set looks like Table 4. All variables from the Health_Chart data set are read in, BMI is calculated from Height and Weight, and then only Patient_ID and BMI are kept, dropping all other variables from the BMI data set.

3.4 OUTPUT Statements

When you run a DATA step in SAS, there is an implicit OUTPUT statement at the end of each step that writes out the contents of the PDV to the specified data set(s). However, you can use one or more explicit OUTPUT statements in your code if you would like to control when and where each row is written to the output table(s). This could be done with a series of IF-THEN statements or within a DO loop to write out each iteration of the loop. If an explicit OUTPUT statement is used, this overrides the implicit OUTPUT statement at the end of the DATA step.

This example utilizes explicit OUTPUT statements to create four data tables through a series of IF-THEN statements. It splits patients in the Health_Chart table up into four different data tables based on classifications resulting from the BMI calculation. One table is created for each of the following BMI classifications: Underweight (Table 5), Healthy Weight (Table 6), Overweight (Table 7), and Obese (Table 8).

```
data Under Healthy Over Obese;
    set input.Health_Chart (keep=Patient_ID Weight Height);
    BMI=Weight / (Height*Height) * 703;
    drop Weight Height;
    if BMI<18.5 then output Under;
    else if BMI>=18.5 and BMI<25 then output Healthy;
    else if BMI>=25 and BMI <30 then output Over;
    else if BMI>=30 then output Obese;
run;
```

Table 5: Under Data Set

Patient_ID	BMI
4437097	18.28824142

Table 6: Healthy Data Set

Patient_ID	BMI
8727172	23.83050847
6015638	24.04660239
9242748	19.95121173
6417249	22.70773001

Table 7: Over Data Set

Patient_ID	BMI
1135601	26.92265054
3651067	26.95945946
9462800	25.97194444

Table 8: Obese Data Set

Patient_ID	BMI
9364322	38.37750772

The following example is a bit trickier because it uses a DO loop. A **DO loop** tells SAS to execute the same statement repeatedly until it reaches the number of times you have specified or reaches the condition that you specified for it to stop executing.

Suppose I have decided to take a road trip from Florida to the Grand Canyon. I have a year to save money and plan to put $175 a month into a vacation checking account. The following code creates a table called Vacation that sets a new variable called Vacation_Fund to 0. It then tells SAS to iterate through the data 12 times (representing each month of my year time frame), adding $175 each time. The explicit OUTPUT statement tells SAS to write out a row for each iteration of the loop, while the FORMAT statement tells SAS that the Vacation_Fund variable is currency and should be formatted with a dollar sign in front and no decimal places.

```
data Vacation;
     Vacation_Fund=0;
     do Deposit=1 to 12;
          Vacation_Fund=Vacation_Fund+175;
          output;
     end;
     format Vacation_Fund dollar10.;
run;
```

When I run this code, SAS will output a row for each iteration of this DO loop, which stands for each month I deposit another $175 into my account. The resulting table is Table 9.

Table 9: Vacation Data Set with Explicit OUTPUT Statement

Vacation_Fund	Deposit
$175	1
$350	2
$525	3
$700	4
$875	5
$1,050	6
$1,225	7
$1,400	8
$1,575	9
$1,750	10
$1,925	11
$2,100	12

This shows that I will have $2,100 saved for my Grand Canyon trip if I save $175 a month for a year. If I were to run the same code without the OUTPUT statement, then SAS would only process a single, implicit OUTPUT statement at the end of the DATA step, and I would only get one row of output, which is the final calculation after SAS has looped through the data 12 times.

```
data Vacation;
     Vacation_Fund=0;
     do Deposit=1 to 12;
          Vacation_Fund=Vacation_Fund+175;
     end;
     format Vacation_Fund dollar10.;
run;
```

Table 10: Vacation Data Set without Explicit OUTPUT Statement

Vacation_Fund	Deposit
$2,100	13

Notice in Table 10 that the $2,100 number is correct. That is the final amount I will have saved for my vacation after a year of deposits. However, the Deposit number looks off. It is 13 instead of 12. That is because when SAS is finished with a DO loop iteration, it increases the iteration by 1 and then loops through the data again. So, after the 12th iteration, SAS increased the Deposit value to 13 but then did not run through the DO loop again as 13 is higher than the specified value of 12. The explicit OUTPUT statement inside the DO loop allows us to see what is happening during each loop and avoids the confusion the implicit OUTPUT statement would cause if the explicit OUTPUT were removed from the DATA step.

Note: If I lost you in the discussion above, don't worry. We have not covered most of this material yet. But I wanted you to see a more complex example of an explicit OUTPUT statement so that you would understand how versatile and useful it can be. You can always revisit this section later.

3.5 SAS Libraries

A **SAS library** is "a collection of one or more SAS files that are recognized by SAS and can be referenced and stored as a unit. Each file is a member of the library."[7] In other words, a SAS library is a location that holds SAS files. A **LIBREF** is the name that you designate for the library that points to the location where these data files are stored. Most LIBREFS point to a folder on your computer or a server that you have access to that contains permanent data files. However, a LIBREF can also point to a location that holds temporary files that are deleted when your SAS session has ended. Anytime you create a table in a SAS program and do not save it to a location as a permanent file or do not specify a LIBREF, SAS saves these tables in a temporary library called WORK. That way, if you reference the table farther down in your program, SAS can find and access the table. But as soon as you close out of your SAS session, the WORK library tables are all deleted. You will need to rerun the SAS program to create these WORK tables again if you need them in the future.

If you assign a LIBREF to a location on your computer or a server and save a table to this LIBREF location, you create a permanent file that you can access at any time. This is helpful because you do not have to rerun the program that created the permanent file or SAS table in the future (unless it needs to be updated). However, saving every table that you create in a SAS program can take up a lot of space on your computer/server and takes more time to read in than a table housed in the WORK library. When I code, my programs typically start by reading in the

---

[7] https://documentation.sas.com/doc/en/pgmsascdc/9.4_3.5/basess/n0a43pssblhvu0n1b51enwlu24n5.htm

permanent file(s) I am working with, then all of the calculations, merges, and data manipulations are completed in WORK tables, and then one or more permanent files are saved out at the end of the program that I will need for reporting purposes or to reference later in other SAS programs.

It is helpful (but not required) to have separate libraries and LIBREFS for your input and output data files. This is a good data practice to help prevent you from accidentally overwriting any input data files. To assign a library:

1. Start with the LIBNAME statement.
2. Create a name for your library (this is the LIBREF).
   a. Note that the LIBREF can be a maximum of 8 characters.
3. Include the path to this library. This path should be enclosed in quotation marks.

You do not need to include the RUN statement at the end as this is not part of a DATA or PROC step.

```
LIBNAME Libref 'path';
```

A LIBREF remains active until you clear it, delete it, or end your SAS session. To clear a library, use the following syntax:

```
LIBNAME Libref CLEAR;
```

For example, let's say I have a folder on my desktop called Book_Data with one subfolder called Input_Data that has all the tables I want to read into SAS and use for the examples in this book and another subfolder called Output_Data where I want to save out the permanent files with the results of these examples. I want the LIBREF for my Input_Data folder to be called INPUT and the LIBREF for my Output_Data folder to be called OUTPUT[8]. To do this, I would want to create two libraries at the beginning of my SAS program.

```
LIBNAME input 'C:\Users\Kirby\Desktop\Book_Data\Input_Data';
LIBNAME output 'C:\Users\Kirby\Desktop\Book_Data\Output_Data';
```

Now, I can reference the INPUT library when I am reading in a source file, and I can reference the OUTPUT library when I want to save out a permanent file.

```
data output.Health_Formatted;
    set input.Health_Chart;
    Eye_Color=upcase(Eye_Color);
run;
```

---

[8] Make sure you have write access permission to the folder that you want to output or export your data tables to, or you will get an error.

This code reads in a SAS table called Health_Chart from the INPUT library, uppercases all values for Eye_Color in the data table, and then saves out a permanent SAS table called Health_Formatted in the OUTPUT library folder.

Here is another example. The following code reads in a permanent SAS table called Survey from the C:\Users\kirby\Desktop\book_data\input_data folder and creates a temporary WORK table called Survey.

```
data Survey;
    Set input.Survey;
run;
```

SAS interfaces typically have a navigation pane where you can view your established libraries (including the WORK library) and view and open the tables in each library. You will also see another default library provided by SAS, SASHELP, listed in the navigation pane. This library contains sample data used in many of the examples provided in SAS documentation. Unlike the WORK library, these files are not deleted and appear each time you open a SAS session.

3.5.1 Macro Libraries

While using LIBREFS is relatively straightforward with SAS data tables, you can run into issues when trying to use LIBREFS when importing and exporting data in other file formats. This is because SAS does not read LIBREF references when they are inside of quotation marks. To get around this issue, you can write out the entire file pathway or turn your library pathway into a macro variable. I wish I had known how to use this trick my first day of coding. Unlike LIBREFS, macro variables can still be read inside of double quotation marks. We will cover more about Macro Variables later as they are an advanced topic. But essentially, macros are shorthand that can make your code more dynamic and efficient.

In this example, you can think of a macro variable as word substitution. Every time SAS comes across a macro variable, it substitutes that word for the text that you specify when creating the macro variable. Use the %LET statement to name your macro variable, and then tell SAS what text to use in place of that word when SAS encounters the word in your program.

```
%let input = C:\Users\Kirby\Desktop\Book_Data\Input_Data;
%let output = C:\Users\Kirby\Desktop\Book_Data\Output_Data;
```

This code creates a macro variable called Input that will be replaced with the text[9] of the pathway to my Input_Data folder when encountered in my program and a macro variable

---

[9] It is best practice never to enclose the text of your macro variable in quotation marks when you create it (i.e., in your %LET statement). Since SAS can recognize macro variables inside of double quotation marks when you run your code, use any required quotation marks when calling the macro (i.e., "&input.") rather than in your %LET statement when creating the macro variable.

called Output with the location of my Output_Data folder. You can name your macro variable something different from your LIBREF name, but I like to name them the same thing since they are referencing the same location.

Note: In SAS, an ampersand (&) marks the start of a macro variable, and a period (.) denotes the end of the macro variable. When SAS encounters a macro variable, it replaces the variable text with the text that was specified earlier on the right-hand side of the equal sign in the %LET statement.

You can use the macro variable that you created to reference the library location when coding inside of quotation marks, like reading in an Excel file (or importing/exporting any data file that is not a SAS table). We will talk more about imports and exports in the next section (Import/ Export). In this example, I am importing the sheet Claim from an Excel file called Read In Data.xlsx from the C:\Users\kirby\Desktop\book_data\input_data folder and saving a temporary table in the WORK library called Ouch.

```
proc import OUT=Ouch
     DATAFILE= "&input.\Read In Data.xlsx"
     DBMS=xlsx REPLACE;
     SHEET="Claim";
     GETNAMES=YES;
run;
```

Here, SAS substitutes the &input. macro variable text with the text used when creating the input macro. This means the DATAFILE= option now reads C:\Users\Kirby\Desktop\Book_Data\Input_ Data\Read In Data.xlsx.

3.5.2 Read-Only Access Libraries

Many companies store data files on servers that multiple employees can access and use simultaneously. Employees often want to read in this data, manipulate and/or merge it with other data, and output a new data file to a different folder without altering the shared source/ input file(s). It is ***extremely easy to accidentally overwrite source files*** when learning to code and working with data files. Most companies (but not all) have backup files or recovery options for when this happens (whew!!). Still, reaching out and telling people what happened is time-consuming, annoying, and embarrassing.

To avoid this, I have implemented an approach I call "saving myself from myself." When I set the LIBNAME for a library that contains source files that I do not want to change, I tell SAS to give me Read-Only access to this folder. That way, I can read in data files and work with them in SAS, but I cannot save out files to that folder or overwrite any files in that folder. Once I've completed all my merges and calculations, I save my final files to a ***different*** folder that I have Write access to.

To do this, you can tell SAS at the beginning of the session that you want to have Read-Only access to a particular folder for the duration of the session. This ends when you close your session, so if you ever need to write something to the source file library, do not run the Read-Only access script during that session. Here is the code for giving yourself Read-Only access to a source file library during your SAS session.

```
libname SF 'C:\Users\Kirby\Desktop\Book_Data\Input_Data'
ACCESS=READONLY;
```

SF is the LIBREF for the same folder location that holds the book data on my desktop. Now, if I try to write out a file to the SF library, I will get an error message (Figure 14).

Figure 14: Read Only Library Error

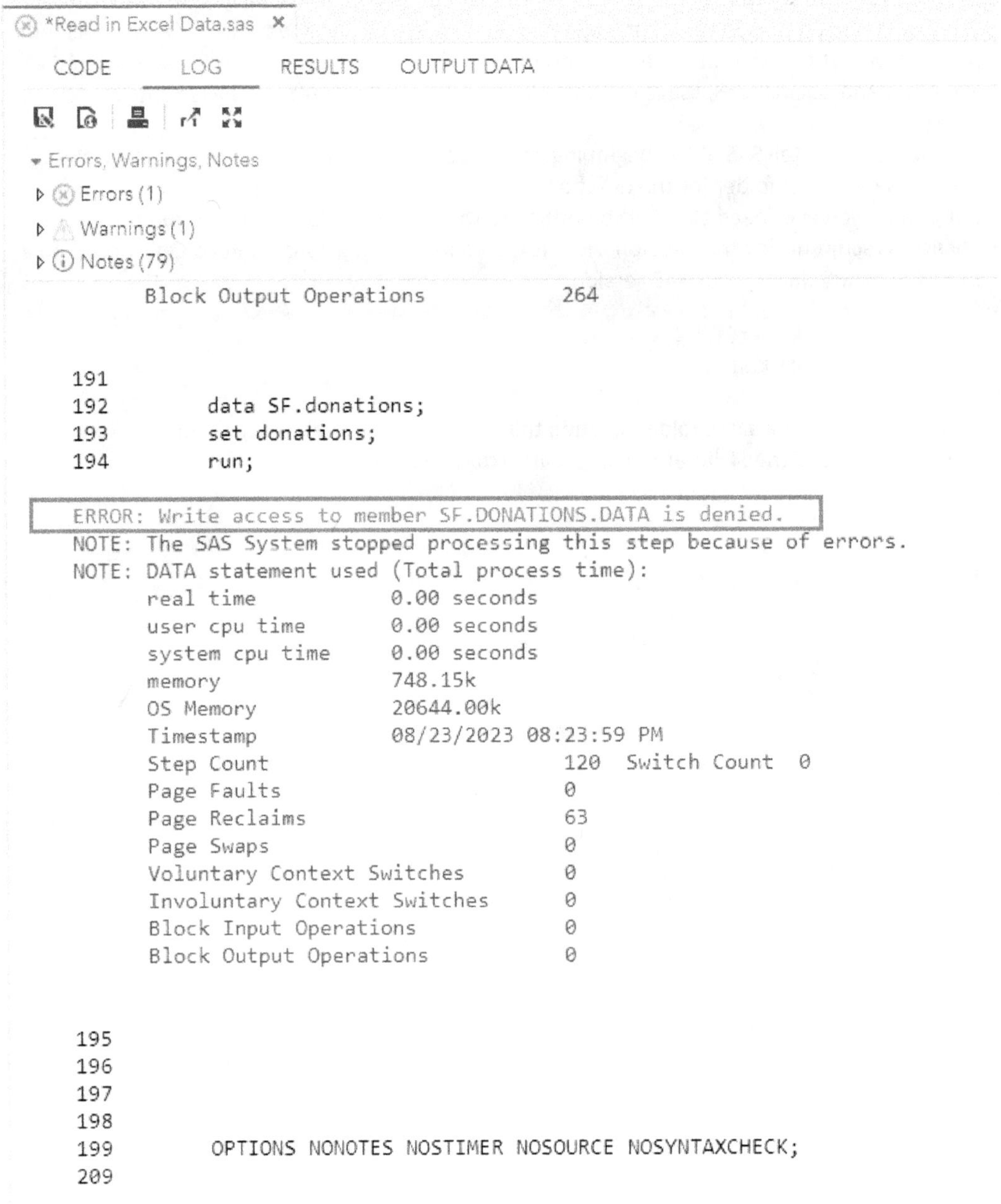

```
⊗ *Read in Excel Data.sas   ✕

    CODE      LOG      RESULTS    OUTPUT DATA

  ▣  ▣  ▤  ↗  ⤢

▾ Errors, Warnings, Notes
▷ ⊗ Errors (1)
▷ ⚠ Warnings (1)
▷ ⓘ Notes (79)
          Block Output Operations            264


    191
    192        data SF.donations;
    193        set donations;
    194        run;

    ERROR: Write access to member SF.DONATIONS.DATA is denied.
    NOTE: The SAS System stopped processing this step because of errors.
    NOTE: DATA statement used (Total process time):
          real time              0.00 seconds
          user cpu time          0.00 seconds
          system cpu time        0.00 seconds
          memory                 748.15k
          OS Memory              20644.00k
          Timestamp              08/23/2023 08:23:59 PM
          Step Count                        120  Switch Count  0
          Page Faults                       0
          Page Reclaims                     63
          Page Swaps                        0
          Voluntary Context Switches        0
          Involuntary Context Switches      0
          Block Input Operations            0
          Block Output Operations           0


    195
    196
    197
    198
    199        OPTIONS NONOTES NOSTIMER NOSOURCE NOSYNTAXCHECK;
    209
```

4 Import/Export

This section describes how to import data files into SAS and export data files from SAS that are in different file formats. SAS data tables have the file extension .sas7bdat and can be read in and saved out as permanent files easily using the LIBREF.Table-Name combination. Files with other extensions like Excel (XLSX) and text (TXT) must be imported and exported differently since they are formatted differently than SAS data tables. The options specified in your import and export code tell SAS how the data in the files is formatted and how SAS needs to transform the data to get it into the SAS format when reading it in or how to export it into a different file format when saving it out as a permanent file.

4.1 Importing Data

Reading data of a different file type and format into SAS is one of the most common yet trickiest things that we do in SAS. Different options are available in PROC IMPORT statements depending on the file type you are reading in. There are many problems I run into frequently during SAS imports. I discuss some common import options and pitfalls to avoid below.

When importing data files, several options can be included to tell SAS about the file type, location, and format of the file that you would like to read in. The DBMS option identifies the file type. The OUT= option specifies the name and location of the SAS output table once the data is read in. The REPLACE option can be included if you'd like to overwrite a SAS table if it already exists.

A delimiter is one or more characters that indicate the boundary between one data field (variable) and the next. The DELIMITER= option tells SAS what character(s) in the file represent this boundary. Files are frequently tab (DELIMITER = '09'x or '05'x on mainframes) or comma delimited (DELIMITER = ',') but can be delimited by other characters like the pipe delimiter '|'. SAS assumes that column names are in the first line of a text file and that data begins on the second line. Options can be included to tell SAS to start reading data at a specific row number, whether to read in variable names, etc. If no delimiter is specified, SAS assumes that the space character is the delimiter.

An issue I frequently encounter when importing data is that SAS truncates (cuts off) data values when reading in a file because the GUESSINGROWS= option is set too low. The GUESSINGROWS= option tells SAS how many table rows to scan before determining whether a column should be classified as numeric or character and the appropriate length to set for the values in a column. It starts at row one and looks through the number of rows specified (the default number is 20) to see whether there are any character constants in the data values of a column and what the longest value is for each column in the observations surveyed. If your data set has longer values lower down in the data set that were not scanned, these values will be truncated to the length that SAS guessed as the longest value based on what was scanned.

To get around this, you can increase the GUESSINGROWS= option number, but this significantly slows down performance/processing time when reading in very large data sets. If you know what length a variable should be in a large data set, a trick is to run the import code on a small number of guessing rows. Next, copy the output in your log that displays the best guess at the variable names, types, and lengths based on what was read in, and paste this output into your editor. Then, manually adjust the names, types, and/or lengths for those variables to what you know they should be. By doing this, you are manually telling SAS how to set up the PDV so that it has the proper names and lengths of the variables that you are reading in. If you now run this adjusted code in your data editor, the code will run much faster because you have hardcoded information for SAS, and it does not have to scan any rows to guess at this information. It just starts writing out one observation at a time based on the parameters that you have specified. This makes importing time much faster for large files. But keep in mind that this code will need to be adjusted if there are any future changes to the file that you are importing, like additional variables being added or columns being saved in a different order. Hardcoding (manually specifying) variable names, types, and lengths is a huge boost to efficiency when reading in large data tables, but you lose out on the flexibility that the PROC IMPORT with GUESSINGROWS has to offer as this method will notice and account for changes in the read in file in the future if you run the code again.

Option 1: Dynamic CSV Import with GUESSINGROWS

```
proc import datafile = "&input.\Bills.csv"
     out = Eww
     dbms = CSV replace;
     guessingrows=5000;
run;
```

Option 2: Static CSV Import with Hardcoded Values

```
data WORK.EWW    ;
%let _EFIERR_ = 0;
     infile "&input.\Bills.csv" delimiter = ',' MISSOVER
     DSD lrecl=13106 firstobs=2 ;
          informat Monthly_Bills $9. ;
          informat Amount best32. ;
          format Monthly_Bills $9. ;
          format Amount best12. ;
     input
          Monthly_Bills  $
          Amount
     ;
     if _ERROR_ then call symputx('_EFIERR_',1);
run;
```

Another common issue is that variable names in the imported file are not in the format accepted by SAS. For example, a variable name in Excel might contain spaces, start with a number, or contain a special character. SAS will read in these variable names exactly the way they appear in the Excel spreadsheet. But then you run into problems in your code when you try to reference these invalid variable names. There are three ways to fix this issue:

1. You can manually edit the external data file that you are reading in to only contain valid SAS variable names (i.e., no more than 32 characters, start with a letter or underscore, and no special characters or spaces). However, this is not recommended as it is tedious and time-consuming, especially if you have a lot of variables in the file that you are importing. Also, you might need to rerun the code every month or year with updated data, which would require manually editing the variable names in your input files every time you rerun the code.
2. My preferred option is using the VALIDVARNAME=V7 option in your import. This option tells SAS to replace any invalid characters with an underscore. For example, the variable name 2002 becomes _2002. The variable Mary's BP Readings becomes Mary_s_BP_Readings. If a variable name looks cluttered with all the underscores when you read it in, you can always use a RENAME statement to make it more user-friendly (e.g., RENAME=(Mary_s_BP_Readings=MarysBP)). V7 is the default VALIDVARNAME system option, so it does not have to be specified in the VALIDVARNAME statement in the program.
3. There are cases where you might not want to change the invalid variable name from the import file because you are exporting the data back into the same format after your calculations or because the resulting table will be used in code or programs down the line that reference the original invalid variable names. If the variable names are changed, it could break code farther down the line that calls variables that no longer exist because they have been renamed. In this case, SAS has a cheat where you can signal it to use the invalid name[10] by enclosing the variable name in double (or single) quotation marks followed by the letter n. For example, if you tell SAS to do a frequency of Mary's BP Readings, you will get an error. However, if you tell it to do a frequency of "Mary's BP Readings"n, it will run the code. Magic.

Option 1: Edit variable names in Excel

Open the Excel file and edit the column names to fit SAS variable naming conventions.

Option 2a: VALIDVARNAME option

```
options VALIDVARNAME=V7;
proc import OUT=coffee
     DATAFILE= "&input.\Read In Data.xlsx"
     DBMS=xlsx REPLACE;
```

---

[10] If the VALIDVARNAME statement has been used, you will need to specify VALIDVARNAME=ANY for SAS to import invalid variable names. Otherwise, SAS will default to the VALIDVARNAME=V7 option and attempt to fix your invalid variable names.

```
            SHEET="Office Coffee Orders";
            GETNAMES=YES;
    run;
    proc freq data=coffee;
        table afternoon_favorites_;
    run;
```

Option 2b: VALIDVARNAME option with a RENAME statement

```
    options VALIDVARNAME=V7;
    proc import OUT=coffee (rename=(Afternoon_Favorites_ = Afternoon_Favs))
        DATAFILE= "&input.\Read In Data.xlsx"
        DBMS=xlsx REPLACE;
        SHEET="Office Coffee Orders";
        GETNAMES=YES;
    run;
    proc freq data=coffee;
        table Afternoon_Favs;
    run;
```

Option 3: Use invalid variable names in code

```
    options VALIDVARNAME=ANY;
    proc import OUT=Coffee
        DATAFILE= "&input.\Read In Data.xlsx"
        DBMS=xlsx REPLACE;
        SHEET="Office Coffee Orders";
        GETNAMES=YES;
    run;

    proc freq data=coffee;
        table 'afternoon favorites!'n;
    run;
```

Another frustrating adventure is reading in fixed-width files. Especially when there are no variable names in the file. When reading in these files, you must tell SAS the starting position for each variable before the variable name and format. Here is an example.

Fixed-Width:

```
    data Plants;
        INFILE "&input.\Plants_Ive_Killed.txt"
        firstobs=1 /*Row to start reading in data values from. */
        obs=MAX /*Use a smaller number to scan the data or use MAX for
    all records */
        LRECL=5000  /*Sets # of characters to read across a row */
        ENCODING="WLATIN1" /*Overrides current SAS session encoding to
    data set encoding */
        NOPAD /*Character strings do not get padded spaces */
```

```
        TRUNCOVER /*Use if any variables may contain missing values*/ ;
        INPUT
                @1    Plant_Name  $20.
                @21   Store    $27.
                @48   Date_Bought  yymmdd8.
                @56   Date_Died  yymmdd8.
    ;
    format Date_Bought Date_Died  mmddyy10.;
    run;
```

Finally, here are some import examples for other file types. Make sure to download the template from https://support.sas.com/en/books/authors/kirby-thomas.html and add your own!

Tab Delimited:

```
    proc import datafile="&input.\GroceryList.txt"
        out=food
        dbms=dlm
        replace;
        delimiter='09'x;
    run;
```

SPSS:

```
    proc import out=gss_imp
        datafile="&input.\GSS7218_R3.sav"
        dbms=SAV replace;
    run;
```

4.2 Exporting Data

When exporting your results table from SAS to another file format, you will typically use a PROC EXPORT statement. The DATA= option names the SAS table to export. The OUTFILE= option tells SAS where to save the permanent table, the name of the file, and the file extension. You can use the DBMS= and REPLACE options the same way they were used in the imports above. Make sure the output file is closed on your computer before you run your export replace code to update that file. Generally speaking, I have experienced fewer issues when exporting data files than importing files into SAS, so I do not have any cautionary advice. However, many people like to format their exported tables/output and make them super fancy by controlling the font, colors, size, etc. See the Reporting section of the guide for more details about how to do this.

For the examples in this section, files will be written out to my Output_Data subfolder. Make sure to update the location of your library to reflect what folder you would like your output files to be saved to. See the SAS Libraries section for more information about setting up SAS libraries.

```
    %let output=C:\Users\Kirby\Desktop\Book_Data\Output_Data;
    libname output "&output.";
```

Here are some basic Export examples that output SAS data tables into other file formats without fancy formatting:

Excel:

```
proc export DATA=input.claim
       OUTFILE= "&output.\Claim_Data.xlsx"
       DBMS=XLSX REPLACE;
       SHEET="Medical";
run;
```

Fun fact: If you want to output several tables as separate tabs in the same Excel workbook, keep the OUTFILE= information the same but change the name in the SHEET= option to a different name. This creates a new sheet/tab in the workbook you already created in your previous PROC EXPORT statement. But make sure the Excel workbook is closed before running the next export procedure.

CSV:

```
proc export data=input.claim
       outfile="&output.\medical_claims.csv"
       dbms=csv replace;
run;
```

Fixed Width :

```
data _null_;
set input.Claim;
file "&output.\Claim_Fixed_Width.txt"
       LRECL=500
       ENCODING="WLATIN1"
       NOPAD;
put
       @1        PatientID  $9.
       @10       ClaimID $11.
       @21       Ctype   3.
       @24       Date    mmddyy10.
       @34       Claim_Desc $35.
       ;
run;
```

Tab Delimited:

```
proc export DATA=input.Claim
       OUTFILE= "&output.\Claim_Tab_Delimited.txt"
       DBMS=tab REPLACE;
run;
```

5 Viewing and Summarizing Data

Once you've read your data into SAS, viewing and summarizing your data is a good first step to understanding what's currently in the data set you are working with and what changes are needed. This step also helps you identify missing or inaccurate data so that you can determine what data cleaning steps should be taken to prepare the data for analysis. The examples throughout this section use data from the General Social Survey (GSS), which can be downloaded at: https://gss.norc.org/get-the-data. The GSS is a project of the independent research organization NORC at the University of Chicago, with principal funding from the National Science Foundation.

This is a large data set (with over 60,000 records and 6,000 variables) that is periodically updated. To ensure you can replicate the results in this section, I have saved a static, formatted, version of this data set with selected variables of interest that can be downloaded from https://support.sas.com/en/books/authors/kirby-thomas.html. You can use this data set to follow along with all of the examples below. To view the code on how this SAS data set was created, see Appendix B: Create GSS SAS Data Set.

5.1 Viewing Data

The PRINT procedure lists the columns and rows of a data table. By default, it lists all columns and rows, which you can also find in the Output Data tab when you read in a file to SAS. This is not always practical when dealing with large data sets. However, when paired with the OBS= option and VAR statement, it can be a great tool to see what information you're working with. The OBS= option enables you to limit the number of rows printed. For example, OBS=10 prints only the first 10 rows of a data set (Table 11). The VAR statement tells SAS which specific variables you want to see in the results window. Also, you might want to add a WHERE statement to your PROC PRINT so that you can examine certain data rows that meet a specified condition, like WHERE Year=1988, Marital="MARRIED", and Age=25 (Table 12).

```
proc print Data=input.GSS (OBS=10);
    VAR YEAR ID AGE MARITAL WRKSTAT SEX PARTYID;
run;
```

Table 11: PROC PRINT First 10 Observations

Obs	YEAR	ID	AGE	MARITAL	WRKSTAT	SEX	PARTYID
1	1972	1	23	NEVER MARRIED	WORKING FULLTIME	FEMALE	IND,NEAR DEM
2	1972	2	70	MARRIED	RETIRED	MALE	NOT STR DEMOCRAT
3	1972	3	48	MARRIED	WORKING PARTTIME	FEMALE	INDEPENDENT
4	1972	4	27	MARRIED	WORKING FULLTIME	FEMALE	NOT STR DEMOCRAT
5	1972	5	61	MARRIED	KEEPING HOUSE	FEMALE	STRONG DEMOCRAT
6	1972	6	26	NEVER MARRIED	WORKING FULLTIME	MALE	IND,NEAR DEM
7	1972	7	28	DIVORCED	WORKING FULLTIME	MALE	IND,NEAR DEM
8	1972	8	27	NEVER MARRIED	WORKING FULLTIME	MALE	IND,NEAR DEM
9	1972	9	21	NEVER MARRIED	WORKING PARTTIME	FEMALE	STRONG DEMOCRAT
10	1972	10	30	MARRIED	WORKING FULLTIME	FEMALE	STRONG DEMOCRAT

```
proc print data=input.GSS;
     WHERE year=1988 and marital="MARRIED" and Age=25;
     VAR YEAR ID AGE MARITAL SEX CLASS;
run;
```

Table 12: PROC PRINT with WHERE Statement

Obs	YEAR	ID	AGE	MARITAL	SEX	CLASS
21947	1988	72	25	MARRIED	MALE	WORKING CLASS
21959	1988	84	25	MARRIED	FEMALE	MIDDLE CLASS
22119	1988	244	25	MARRIED	FEMALE	MIDDLE CLASS
22123	1988	248	25	MARRIED	MALE	MIDDLE CLASS
22324	1988	449	25	MARRIED	MALE	WORKING CLASS
22425	1988	550	25	MARRIED	MALE	MIDDLE CLASS
22621	1988	746	25	MARRIED	FEMALE	WORKING CLASS
22688	1988	813	25	MARRIED	MALE	WORKING CLASS
22711	1988	836	25	MARRIED	FEMALE	MIDDLE CLASS
22723	1988	848	25	MARRIED	MALE	MIDDLE CLASS
22863	1988	988	25	MARRIED	MALE	LOWER CLASS
22990	1988	1115	25	MARRIED	FEMALE	MIDDLE CLASS
23078	1988	1203	25	MARRIED	FEMALE	WORKING CLASS
23183	1988	1308	25	MARRIED	MALE	WORKING CLASS
23200	1988	1325	25	MARRIED	FEMALE	WORKING CLASS

The UNIVARIATE procedure prints summary statistics for every numeric variable in your data set, such as N, mean, median, mode, standard deviation, variance, skewness, and extreme values. You can limit the number of variables included in the results by selecting variables of interest in the VAR statement. There are additional options that you can use to add graphics, calculate percentiles, etc. Table 13 displays the results of running a PROC UNIVARIATE on the Age variable in the GSS data set.

```
proc univariate Data=input.GSS;
      VAR Age;
run;
```

Table 13: PROC UNIVARIATE of Age Variable in the GSS

The UNIVARIATE Procedure

Variable: AGE (Age of respondent)

Moments			
N	64586	Sum Weights	64586
Mean	46.0993559	Sum Observations	2977373
Std Deviation	17.5347031	Variance	307.465811
Skewness	0.41481013	Kurtosis	-0.7741985
Uncorrected SS	157112657	Corrected SS	19857679.4
Coeff Variation	38.0367637	Std Error Mean	0.06899684

Basic Statistical Measures			
Location		Variability	
Mean	46.09936	Std Deviation	17.5347
Median	44	Variance	307.46581
Mode	30	Range	71
		Interquartile Range	28

Tests for Location: Mu0=0				
Test	Statistic		p Value	
Student's t	t	668.1372	Pr > |t|	<.0001
Sign	M	32293	Pr >= |M|	<.0001
Signed Rank	S	1.04E+09	Pr >= |S|	<.0001

Quantiles (Definition 5)	
Level	Quantile
100% Max	89
99%	86
95%	78
90%	72
75% Q3	59
50% Median	44
25% Q1	31
10%	24
5%	22
1%	19
0% Min	18

Extreme Observations			
Lowest		Highest	
Value	Obs	Value	Obs
18	64538	89	64264
18	64521	89	64545
18	64408	89	64611
18	64344	89	64735
18	64304	89	64807

Missing Values			
Missing	Count	Percent Of	
Value		All Obs	Missing Obs
.	228	0.35	100

5.2 Summarizing Data

The MEANS procedure outputs basic summary statistics like mean, max, min, and range for numeric variables. You can select which variables you want the summary statistics calculated for in the VAR statement. You can also add a CLASS statement if you would like the statistics calculated separately for each group of another variable. For example, if I want the summary statistics for Age in my data set but want the results reported separately based on Sex, I would specify Age in the VAR statement and Sex in the CLASS statement (Table 14).

```
proc means data=input.GSS;
    VAR Age;
    CLASS Sex;
run;
```

Table 14: PROC MEANS of Age by Sex in GSS

	Analysis Variable : AGE of respondent					
SEX	N Obs	N	Mean	Std Dev	Minimum	Maximum
FEMALE	36200	36044	46.64199	17.86597	18	89
MALE	28614	28542	45.41409	17.08291	18	89

The FREQ procedure displays how many times a specific value occurs in the data set for each variable listed in the TABLES statement. For example, if I run a PROC FREQ on the variable PartyID, the output table would tell me how many people in my data set were Democrats (strong versus not strong), Republicans (strong versus not strong), Independents (leaning Democrat, leaning Republican, or true Independents), or Other (Table 15). Be careful not to run a PROC FREQ on a variable with many different values, especially numbers with decimal places. SAS outputs each value that it finds in a column and counts how many times that value appears. This is super helpful with character variables with 20 or fewer discrete categories. However, SAS can stop processing and write an error message in the log if you ask it to run a frequency on a variable with over 100 different categories.

```
proc freq data=input.GSS;
    TABLES PartyID;
run;
```

Table 15: PROC FREQ of PartyID Variable in GSS

PARTYID	Frequency	Percent	Cumulative Frequency	Cumulative Percent
IND,NEAR DEM	7792	12.1	7792	12.1
IND,NEAR REP	5721	8.88	13513	20.98
INDEPENDENT	9888	15.35	23401	36.34
NOT STR DEMOCRAT	13294	20.64	36695	56.98
NOT STR REPUBLICAN	9933	15.42	46628	72.41
OTHER PARTY	1072	1.66	47700	74.07
STRONG DEMOCRAT	10378	16.12	58078	90.19
STRONG REPUBLICAN	6318	9.81	64396	100
Frequency Missing = 418				

The TABULATE procedure is helpful if you'd like to produce two- or three-dimensional tables. Perhaps you are interested in how Party ID differs by Sex. To create a table that has rows for each PartyID and columns for Sex, use the TABULATE procedure and list PartyID and Sex in the CLASS and TABLE statements (Table 16). Dimensions in PROC TABULATE are delimited by a comma. Whichever variable you specify first (before the comma) in a two-dimensional TABLE statement will be the row variable, while the second variable (after the comma) will be the column variable.

```
proc tabulate data=input.GSS;
      CLASS PartyID Sex;
      TABLE PartyID, Sex;
run;
```

Table 16: PROC TABULATE of PartyID by Sex in GSS

	SEX	
	FEMALE	MALE
	N	N
PARTYID		
IND,NEAR DEM	4086	3706
IND,NEAR REP	2716	3005
INDEPENDENT	5561	4327
NOT STR DEMOCRAT	8084	5210
NOT STR REPUBLICAN	5468	4465
OTHER PARTY	479	593
STRONG DEMOCRAT	6244	4134
STRONG REPUBLICAN	3312	3006

Let's say you would like to further distinguish your results by Race. You would need to create a three-dimensional table. To do this, add Race as the first variable in the CLASS and TABLE statements. By specifying Race first in the TABLE statement, you are classifying it as the page variable, while PartyID remains the row variable, and Sex remains the column variable. Table 17 shows that this code prints separate tables for each category of Race by PartyID and Sex.

```
proc tabulate data=input.GSS;
      CLASS PartyID Sex Race;
      TABLE Race, PartyID, Sex;
run;
```

Table 17: PROC TABULATE of PartyID by Sex and Race in GSS (Multiple Tables)

RACE BLACK

	SEX	
	FEMALE	MALE
	N	N
PARTYID		
IND,NEAR DEM	583	489
IND,NEAR REP	160	117
INDEPENDENT	712	450
NOT STR DEMOCRAT	1570	882
NOT STR REPUBLICAN	182	146
OTHER PARTY	49	38
STRONG DEMOCRAT	2246	1301
STRONG REPUBLICAN	94	71

RACE OTHER

	SEX	
	FEMALE	MALE
	N	N
PARTYID		
IND,NEAR DEM	232	254
IND,NEAR REP	117	123
INDEPENDENT	546	441
NOT STR DEMOCRAT	472	367
NOT STR REPUBLICAN	155	163
OTHER PARTY	35	34
STRONG DEMOCRAT	261	190
STRONG REPUBLICAN	74	84

RACE WHITE

PARTYID	SEX FEMALE N	MALE N
IND,NEAR DEM	3271	2963
IND,NEAR REP	2439	2765
INDEPENDENT	4303	3436
NOT STR DEMOCRAT	6042	3961
NOT STR REPUBLICAN	5131	4156
OTHER PARTY	395	521
STRONG DEMOCRAT	3737	2643
STRONG REPUBLICAN	3144	2851

You can use many formatting options with PROC TABULATE to create more complex tables. Two important options include the * symbol to separate multiple column or row variables and the ALL keyword to generate summary statistics for variables in a specific dimension. In this example, the TABLE statement includes PartyID as the row variable and Sex*Race as the two column variables with the keyword ALL. Table 18 shows the resulting table, which displays the same information as Table 17, but in a layout that is easier to read at a glance. Table 18 also includes a summary column called All at the end that contains the total number of people in each PartyID category.

```
proc tabulate data=input.GSS;
     CLASS PartyID Sex Race;
     TABLE PartyID, Sex*Race all;
run;
```

Table 18: PROC TABULATE of PartyID by Sex and Race in GSS (One Table)

	SEX						
	FEMALE			MALE			
	RACE			RACE			
	BLACK	OTHER	WHITE	BLACK	OTHER	WHITE	All
PARTYID	N	N	N	N	N	N	N
IND,NEAR DEM	583	232	3271	489	254	2963	7792
IND,NEAR REP	160	117	2439	117	123	2765	5721
INDEPENDENT	712	546	4303	450	441	3436	9888
NOT STR DEMOCRAT	1570	472	6042	882	367	3961	13294
NOT STR REPUBLICAN	182	155	5131	146	163	4156	9933
OTHER PARTY	49	35	395	38	34	521	1072
STRONG DEMOCRAT	2246	261	3737	1301	190	2643	10378
STRONG REPUBLICAN	94	74	3144	71	84	2851	6318

Part Two: Coding with SAS

6 Data Transformations

Now that you know what your data looks like, you are ready to make changes to your data based on your business needs. Data transformations can include operations like rounding values, creating or calculating new variables, concatenating (combining) two variables into a single new variable, or transforming numeric values into character values.

It is good practice not to overwrite your original variables with the data transformations that you perform. Instead, create a new variable that you can compare against the original variable. This enables you to make sure the transformation worked the way you intended and to make different transformations later using the original variable if someone asks for a change or an additional calculation. You can always drop the original variable from the final data, but at least the variable still exists in your program if you need to make any quick adjustments.

The transformations listed in this section typically occur when working with a single data table. We will talk about merging and combining data tables in another section.

6.1 Sorting and De-duplicating Data

Sorting data is one of the most frequent and useful procedures I use in SAS. Sorting rows enables you to easily visualize your data in an order that makes sense to you and/or the reader of your output. For example, you might want to sort your data file by family name to look up a record for a particular person easily. I often sort data at the end of my DATA steps and then look at the Output Data tab to make sure the DATA step I just ran did what I think I coded it to do.

I also use sorting when I de-duplicate records. De-duplication is extremely useful for removing repeat records, but I use it primarily to identify the primary ID on a table. Every data table should be unique by a single ID field or at least by a combination of several fields in the data set. What I mean by unique is that each row/observation in the data set can be identified by this ID field or variable combination. No other row has the same value (or combination of values) as another row in the ID column(s).

For example, a data set with test scores might be unique by the student ID (each student has a single row in the data set with one column displaying their unique student ID and another representing their test score). A weekly time sheet log, on the other hand, might be unique by employee ID, date, and punch in time. This is because the employee likely clocks in more than once during the week, so you must look at each employee, date, and punch in time to uniquely identify each row in the data set representing a unique punch in. An employee ID does not uniquely identify a record. Nor does the punch in time or date. You need all three fields.

Knowing what variable(s) your table is unique by is imperative if you want to merge it with other data tables later. If you do not use the correct ID fields, you could lose important data or accidentally duplicate or mismatch data pieces that should not go together. ***Understanding what variable(s) a data set is unique by is the most important part of data analytics***. Thank you for coming to my TED Talk.

Now, let's walk through an example together. The code below would take a data set called Claim, sort it by PatientID, Date, and ClaimID, and save the resulting, sorted data set as Claims_Sorted (Table 19). This data set is sorted by PatientID first, meaning all of the records for a patient are now grouped together starting with the patient with the lowest ID number and moving down the list with the second highest number, etc. Then, within each PatientID, the data is sorted by Date, meaning that the claim that occurred first for that patient will occur on the first row, followed by the claim that occurred second, and so on. Adding ClaimID as the last variable in the sort means that if two claims for a patient happened to occur on the same day, the lowest ClaimID is on the first row and the larger ClaimID is on the second row.

```
proc sort data=input.Claim out=Claims_Sorted;
     by PatientID Date ClaimID;
run;
```

Table 19: Claims_Sorted Data Set

PatientID	ClaimID	Ctype	Date	Claim_Desc
221923797	21460513062	755	05/17/2022	Flu Vaccine
567660147	80995718432	177	11/12/2021	Physical Therapy
567660147	86902627542	222	11/12/2021	X-Ray Shoulder
774658165	91833838898	755	05/28/2021	Flu Vaccine
811279234	39343015857	177	09/05/2021	Physical Therapy
811279234	75217985959	300	12/09/2021	MRI Spine
811279234	50564174591	496	03/31/2022	X-Ray Femur
935472958	90557924941	562	10/31/2020	Lipid Panel
935472958	62369319156	41	02/18/2021	Annual Physical Exam

Once the data is sorted, the second PROC SORT runs the NODUPKEY option BY PatientID, meaning that it reads in the Claims_Sorted data and outputs a data set called Claims_ND that only has one record per patient (Table 20). Based on the sort in the previous step, it is keeping only the ***first*** claim for that patient, as the NODUPKEY keeps the first instance (or row) for whatever you de-duplicate by.

```
proc sort data=claims_sorted out=claims_nd nodupkey;
     by PatientID;
run;
```

Table 20: De-duplicated Claims Data Set

PatientID	ClaimID	Ctype	Date	Claim_Desc
221923797	21460513062	755	05/17/2022	Flu Vaccine
567660147	80995718432	177	11/12/2021	Physical Therapy
774658165	91833838898	755	05/28/2021	Flu Vaccine
811279234	39343015857	177	09/05/2021	Physical Therapy
935472958	90557924941	562	10/31/2020	Lipid Panel

If you add Date to the BY statement in the NODUPKEY sort, this will produce a unique list on PatientID and Date, meaning you will have one row for every patient/date combo, but in instances where there were multiple claims in one day, it will only keep the first (lowest ClaimID) claim for the patient on that day.

6.2 Calculating New Variables

When coding, the need often arises to create a new variable based on one or more variables that are already in your data set. For example, you might want to create a new Income variable that copies all values for Income and then replaces missing values with your sample's median Income. Or perhaps you want to calculate a Total column in your data set based on a Price column that you need to multiply by a state's sales tax to get the total cost. There are many ways to create variables in SAS, but the easiest is to define them in a DATA step. Enter your new variable name, =, and the expression needed to calculate the values of the new variable.

In this example, the CATX function combines the First_Name and Last_Name variables, separated by the specified delimiter of space (' '), into one variable called FullName (Table 21). It is good practice to create a new variable name (not already in the data set) so that you do not overwrite any original data values. Also, start with a LENGTH statement when you create a character variable to avoid truncating values. Adding the LENGTH statement before your SET statement will put your newly created variable as the first column of your output data set since you define its characteristics before reading in the input data set. If the LENGTH statement comes after the SET statement (but before you create your variable), then your variable will appear at the end of your data set. Only the variables of interest are kept in the output data set.

```
data Create_Vars (keep=First_name Last_Name FullName);
     Set input.Donations_JUL;
     Length FullName $50.;
     FullName=CATX(' ',First_Name, Last_Name);
run;
```

Table 21: Calculate New Variable Example

First_Name	Last_Name	FullName
John	Brown	John Brown
Kelsey	Green	Kelsey Green
Sherlock	Holmes	Sherlock Holmes

You can also create variables using conditional logic statements in DATA steps and with PROC SQL. See the Conditional Logic section for more information.

6.3 Filtering

The **WHERE** statement is used for filtering rows. If the expression included in this statement is true for a row on the data set you are reading in, SAS outputs the row. If the statement is false for a row on the input data set, that row is excluded and does not appear in the output. Common operators in a WHERE statement include:

- = or EQ (equals)
- ^= or ~= or NE (does not equal)
- > or GT (greater than)
- < or LT (less than)
- >= or GE (greater than or equal to)
- <= or LE (less than or equal to)

Also, the word **NOT**, the ^ symbol, or the ~ symbol can all be used to indicate the opposite of the operator that you use. For example, you might want SAS to keep all records where a variable is NOT equal to missing (e.g., ^= . for numeric variables or ~= ' ' for character variables).

IN is also a very useful operator that enables you to choose a list of values that should be included in the output data set. For example, you could say where ice-cream flavor is chocolate, vanilla, or strawberry. Only the rows with one of these three flavors will be included in your results. All other flavors are excluded. The values must be enclosed in quotation marks if they are character values and should be separated by a space or comma. All values should be enclosed in parentheses. For example, IN (2, 3, 4) for numeric variables or IN ("CHOCOLATE" "VANILLA" "STRAWBERRY") for character variables. The IN operator can be paired with NOT to indicate which rows should not be output.

You can create compound conditions with AND / OR keywords. You would use **AND** or an ampersand if a row must meet all conditions specified in your WHERE statement. You would use **OR** or the symbols | or ! if a row only needs to meet one condition in the list to be included.

This example uses a WHERE statement to include records where the year is equal to 2006, the respondent's age is equal to 32, their degree includes "BACHELOR" or "GRADUATE", and their Class is not equal to missing (Table 22).

```
Data And_Example;
    set input.GSS;
    where year=2006 and age=32 and degree in ("BACHELOR"
    "GRADUATE")and class^=" ";
    drop marital partyid;
run;
```

Table 22: Filtering using WHERE / AND Operator Example

YEAR	ID	AGE	WRKSTAT	DEGREE	SEX	RACE	CLASS
2006	10	32	WORKING FULLTIME	GRADUATE	FEMALE	OTHER	MIDDLE CLASS
2006	86	32	KEEPING HOUSE	GRADUATE	FEMALE	OTHER	MIDDLE CLASS
2006	352	32	WORKING FULLTIME	BACHELOR	FEMALE	OTHER	WORKING CLASS
2006	407	32	WORKING FULLTIME	BACHELOR	FEMALE	WHITE	MIDDLE CLASS
2006	544	32	WORKING FULLTIME	BACHELOR	MALE	OTHER	LOWER CLASS
2006	965	32	UNEMPL, LAID OFF	GRADUATE	FEMALE	BLACK	MIDDLE CLASS
2006	1665	32	WORKING FULLTIME	BACHELOR	FEMALE	WHITE	MIDDLE CLASS
2006	1699	32	WORKING FULLTIME	GRADUATE	MALE	WHITE	MIDDLE CLASS
2006	2097	32	WORKING FULLTIME	BACHELOR	MALE	OTHER	MIDDLE CLASS
2006	2415	32	UNEMPL, LAID OFF	BACHELOR	MALE	WHITE	WORKING CLASS
2006	2563	32	WORKING FULLTIME	BACHELOR	FEMALE	WHITE	WORKING CLASS
2006	2591	32	WORKING FULLTIME	BACHELOR	MALE	OTHER	WORKING CLASS
2006	2859	32	WORKING FULLTIME	BACHELOR	MALE	WHITE	WORKING CLASS
2006	3354	32	KEEPING HOUSE	BACHELOR	FEMALE	WHITE	MIDDLE CLASS
2006	3724	32	WORKING FULLTIME	GRADUATE	FEMALE	WHITE	MIDDLE CLASS
2006	4113	32	WORKING FULLTIME	BACHELOR	MALE	OTHER	WORKING CLASS
2006	4390	32	WORKING FULLTIME	BACHELOR	MALE	WHITE	MIDDLE CLASS

It is important to note that these operators can be used outside of the WHERE statement, like when applying Conditional Logic.

6.4 Conditional Logic

There are times when you want to do calculations only if a certain condition is met. For example, if you wanted to see whether a sample of individuals were eligible to take a follow up survey about their visit, you might want to create a column called Eligible with a value of 1 if the individual is 18 or older and 0 if the person is younger than 18 (Table 23). To accomplish this, you can use an IF-THEN statement.

```
data Eligible_Sample;
     Set input.health_chart;
     IF Age >= 18 THEN Eligible=1;
     ELSE Eligible=0;
run;
```

Table 23: Conditional Logic Example

Patient_ID	Height	Weight	Eye_Color	Age	Eligible
8727172	59	118	blue	21	1
6015638	66	149	green	42	1
9242748	56	89	brown	11	0
1135601	63	152	brown	65	1
3651067	74	210	blue	34	1
4437097	62	100	brown	16	0
6417249	67	145	blue	57	1
9462800	60	133	brown	89	1
9364322	72	283	brown	38	1

In some cases, you might want to do more than one thing if a certain criterion is met. For example, you might want to assign a Language field and a Currency field based on the Country listed in the following data set (Table 24).

Table 24: Travel Destinations Data Set

Country	City	Miles
Usa	Philadelphia	4,117
Usa	Boston	3,837
Germany	Munich	1
Germany	Berlin	363
Kyrgyzstan	Bishkek	4,200
Italy	Rome	587
Austria	Vienna	270

To do this, you would use an IF-THEN DO statement. All DO statements must be accompanied by an END statement to tell SAS to stop processing the DO statement.

In this example, SAS creates a Language variable and a Currency variable. It sets the Language to "English" for the records where the uppercase of Country is "USA" and the Currency to "Dollar". For records where the uppercase of Country is "GERMANY" or "AUSTRIA", SAS sets the Language to "German" and the Currency to "Euro". "ITALY" records are coded as having a Language of

"Italian" and a Currency of "Euro". The ELSE DO statement codes all other records that do not have an uppercase Country value of "USA", "GERMANY", "AUSTRIA", or "ITALY" as "Other" Language and Currency (Table 25).

```
data Travel_Needs;
    set input.Travel_Destinations;
    length Language $25. Currency $15.;

    if upcase(Country) = "USA" then do;
    Language="English";
    Currency="Dollar";
    end;

    else if upcase(Country) in("GERMANY" "AUSTRIA") then do;
    Language="German";
    Currency="Euro";
    end;

    else if upcase(Country) = "ITALY" then do;
    Language="Italian";
    Currency="Euro";
    end;

    else do;
    Language="Other";
    Currency="Other";
    end;
run;
```

Table 25: IF THEN DO Example

Country	City	Miles	Language	Currency
Usa	Philadelphia	4,117	English	Dollar
Usa	Boston	3,837	English	Dollar
Germany	Munich	1	German	Euro
Germany	Berlin	363	German	Euro
Kyrgyzstan	Bishkek	4,200	Other	Other
Italy	Rome	587	Italian	Euro
Austria	Vienna	270	German	Euro

Note: Remember to set a length first if you are creating a character variable with your conditional logic. If you don't, SAS will automatically set the length to the first value generated for the field and truncate any values longer than this.

To apply conditional logic using PROC SQL, you will use a CASE WHEN statement. You will learn more about this syntax in the PROC SQL section. For this example, notice the statement begins with CASE WHEN, defines a condition (Miles < 1), and sets a value for a new variable if that condition is met ("Walk"). It continues with WHEN statements defining other conditions and subsequent values. When the only records left that have not met the criteria of the previous statements should all be coded the same value for the new variable, use the ELSE statement. Once all categories for the new variable have been defined, use the keyword END to signify that there are no more categories and then the AS keyword and the name of your new variable (Transportation). Table 26 displays the results.

```
proc sql;
     create table Travel as
     select *,
     case when Miles <= 1 then 'Walk'
     when Miles >= 600 then 'Fly'
     else 'Drive' end as Transportation
     from input.Travel_Destinations;
quit;
```

Table 26: CASE WHEN Example

Country	City	Miles	Transportation
Usa	Philadelphia	4,117	Fly
Usa	Boston	3,837	Fly
Germany	Munich	1	Walk
Germany	Berlin	363	Drive
Kyrgyzstan	Bishkek	4,200	Fly
Italy	Rome	587	Drive
Austria	Vienna	270	Drive

Remember that you can use all the operators listed in the Filtering section above when creating your conditional logic rules.

6.5 Manipulating Values

SAS has hundreds of functions that enable you to perform calculations on numeric and date values or manipulate character values[11]. When appropriate, functions can be used to turn character values into numeric and numeric values into character. Functions start with the function name (e.g., UPCASE) followed by a set of required and optional arguments separated by commas and enclosed in parentheses. Functions can be used on a single, specified numeric or

---

[11] To find a list of all SAS® functions, visit: https://go.documentation.sas.com/doc/en/pgmsascdc/9.4_3.5/lefunctionsref/p1q8bq2v0o11n6n1gpij335fqpph.htm

character value or applied to all values in a column when you list a variable name as one of your arguments.

Functions are often used when creating new variables based on calculations or manipulations done to one or more original variables in the data set. An example of this would be creating a new variable called Name by taking the uppercase values of a field called Full_Name. If the first observation in your data set has a Full_Name value of "Amy Conner", the new Name column would display "AMY CONNER". Functions are also frequently used in conditional logic. For example, you could use the MISSING function to say that if a value for the variable Income is missing, it should be replaced with the median Income value for the data set.

Functions can also be stacked. This means that you can have a function within a function. The resolved value of the inner function is used as an argument in the outer function. This comes in handy when you need to convert a character variable to numeric before you perform a calculation on the values of that variable. It can also be used to round the calculation results, as you will see in the Manipulating Values section.

6.5.1 Character Functions

Character values (often referred to as strings) are case-sensitive and must be in quotation marks. The following is a list of common functions used to transform or combine character values.

SUBSTR: Returns a portion of a character value based on the start position and length that you specify

SCAN: Returns a section of a character value depending on the delimiter and position that you specify. Positive numbers indicate the word position from left to right, while a negative number represents the word position from right to left.

UPCASE: Makes all letters in a value uppercase

LOWCASE: Makes all letters in a value lowercase

PROPCASE: Makes the first letter in a value uppercase and the rest of the values lowercase

CAT: Concatenates character values and adds a space between them. Does not remove leading or trailing blanks.

CATS: Concatenates character values with no space in between and removes leading and trailing blanks

CATX: Concatenates character values with a custom delimiter that you specify

COMPRESS: Removes specified characters from character value. Default removes spaces, but you can specify a list of characters to remove or use different modifiers to specify all letters, all numbers, punctuation marks, etc.

INPUT: Transforms character values into numeric values. This only works if the character value contains only numeric data.

6.5.2 Numeric Functions

Numeric values are not in quotation marks and must only include digits, decimal points, and negative signs. The following is a list of common functions used in SAS to transform numeric values or make calculations.

SUM: Adds values together

MEAN: Calculates the average (mean)

MEDIAN: Calculates the median

RANGE: Calculates the range

MIN: Calculates the minimum

MAX: Calculates the maximum

ROUND: Rounds numeric values to the decimal point that you specify

PUT: Transforms numeric values into character values

6.5.3 Date Functions

SAS internally records **datetime** values as the number of seconds between midnight, January 1, 1960, and the specified date and time. SAS **date** values are stored internally as the number of days between January 1, 1960, and a specified date. All dates and datetime values are stored as integers that are positive if they occur after January 1, 1960, and negative integers if they occur before this date. We rarely see these integers in our results as dates are typically formatted so that we can easily interpret them.

When an expression includes a fixed date value, use the SAS date constant syntax: "ddmmmyyyy"d, where dd represents a 2-digit day, mmm represents a 3-letter month, and yyyy represents a 2- or 4-digit year. For example, you might want to tell SAS to keep all records after "01JUN2020"d.

The following functions can be used to transform date variables in SAS.

MONTH: Returns a number from 1 to 12 that represents the month

DAY: Returns a number from 1 to 31 that represents the day of the month

YEAR: Returns the 4-digit year

MDY: Returns a SAS date value from the month, day, and year numbers that you input

YRDIF: Calculates the number of years between two dates listed in the first and second arguments. The 'AGE' option should be used in the third argument for a precise age using a birthdate field (first argument) and another date field (second argument—could be the current date or the date of the interview, etc.). The 'ACT/ACT' option uses the actual number of days between the two dates, and then divides the number of days from years with 365 days by 365 and divides the number of days from years with 366 days by 366 to get the year difference. You can also specifically set the number of days in a year to divide by with the 'ACT/360' or 'ACT/365' options, regardless of the actual number of days in a specific calendar year. The '30/60' option calculates the year difference based on an assumed 30-day calendar month and 360-day year.

DATDIF: Calculates the number of days between two dates listed in the first and second arguments. You can use all of the same options as YRDIF in the third argument except for the 'AGE' option.

INTNX: Increments a SAS date by a specified number of intervals. This function can be used to find the date of next Tuesday, a date 24 weeks in the future, to subtract 2 quarters from a date, etc. There can be up to 4 arguments in the INTNX function. The first is the interval, which can be days, weeks, months, quarters, or years. The second argument is the date that you are starting from. The third argument is the number of intervals by which the date should be incremented (can be positive or negative). The fourth and final argument is optional and represents where the date value is aligned within an interval before being incremented. You can specify 'beginning', 'middle', 'end', and 'sameday', though the default is 'beginning'.

6.5.4 Manipulating Values Example

Here is an example that walks through several data transformations. This code reads in a data set called Donations_JUL (Table 27), creates several new variables using data transformations, and outputs a new data set called Transformations (Table 28).

Table 27: Donations_JUL Data Set

First_Name	Last_Name	Address	DOB	Donation	Donation_Date	Merchandise
John	Brown	6523 E Cherry St	5/22/1957	$500	7/12/2022	$122.68
Kelsey	Green	3111 Orange Ave	3/16/1989	$25	7/13/2022	$57.23
Sherlock	Holmes	221B Baker Street	1/6/1977	$221	7/8/2022	$0.00

```
data Transformations;
    set input.Donations_JUL;
    Substr_Ex=substr(Address, 1, 4);
    Scan_Ex=scan(Address, 2, ' ');
    Upcase_Ex=upcase(First_Name);
    Catx_Ex=catx(' ',First_Name, Last_Name);
    Input_Ex=input(compress(Address,' ', 'a'), 8.);
    Sum_Ex=sum(Donation, Merchandise);
    Month_Ex=month(DOB);
    Mdy_Ex=mdy(7,31,2022); /*date of analysis*/
    Yrdif_Ex=round(yrdif(DOB, Mdy_Ex, 'AGE'), .01);
    Datdif_Ex=datdif(Donation_Date, Mdy_Ex, 'ACTUAL');
    Intnx_Ex=intnx('month', Donation_Date, 1, 'SAMEDAY');
    format Mdy_Ex Intnx_Ex mmddyy10.;
run;
```

Table 28: Transformations Data Set (Created Variables Only)

Substr_Ex	Scan_Ex	Upcase_Ex	Catx_Ex	Input_Ex	Sum_Ex	Month_Ex	Mdy_Ex	Yrdif_Ex	Datdif_Ex	Intnx_Ex
6523	E	JOHN	John Brown	6523	622.68	5	7/31/2022	65.19	19	8/12/2022
3111	Orange	KELSEY	Kelsey Green	3111	82.23	3	7/31/2022	33.38	18	8/13/2022
221B	Baker	SHERLOCK	Sherlock Holmes	221	221	1	7/31/2022	45.56	23	8/8/2022

The Substr_Ex variable is created using the SUBSTRING function to extract the first four digits from the Address variable. The function tells SAS to start reading at position 1 and stop reading after 4 characters have been read in.

Next, the Scan_Ex variable is created by using the SCAN function on the Address variable and pulling in the second word. The function specifies that " (the space character) is the delimiter used to separate words in Address. Hence, SAS knows that the second word is the first word after the first space in Address.

The Upcase_Ex variable is created using the UPCASE function on the First_Name variable. This makes all letters in the name capitalized. First_Name and Last_Name are then concatenated using the CATX function with a space delimiter to generate the Catx_Ex variable.

The Input_Ex variable uses the INPUT and COMPRESS functions together to compress out all the upper and lowercase letters in the Address string (in this case leaving only the digits behind) and then inputting those numbers to create a numeric variable rather than a character variable made up of digits.

The code then moves into numeric data transformations. The Sum_Ex variable adds each donor's Donation and Merchandise values to get the total amount spent. The Month_Ex variable uses the MONTH function to extract the month from the donor's DOB, while the MDY function is used to create the variable Mdy_Ex representing the date of the analysis. The Yeardif_Ex variable takes the difference between the date of the analysis (Mdy_Ex) and the donor's birthday (DOB) to calculate the donor's age and then rounds the result to the hundreds place with the ROUND function. The actual number of days between the analysis date (Mdy_Ex) and the Donation_Date is calculated using the DATDIF function, while the INTNX function is used to create a variable (Intnx_Ex) representing one month after the donation date for each donor to indicate when each person should be contacted to request additional donations.

6.6 Formatting

Formats are used to change the way values are ***displayed*** in the data and in reports, but they ***do not change*** the underlying data **values**. Formats are applied using a FORMAT statement and contain a period so that SAS knows it is a format and not a variable name.

There are three generic formats that SAS uses for character, numeric, and date values. In these formats, *w* represents the width of the variable, and *d* indicates the number of decimal places. Character variables are typically in the form *$w.*, numeric variables are typically in the form *w.d*, and date variables are often in the format *MMDDYYw*. Remember, *w* indicates the width, so if a date is in the format *MMDDYY8.*, it will appear as 04/22/21. Alternatively, the format *MMDDYY10.* will be displayed as 04/22/2021 as it allows for a length of ten characters rather than just eight.

There are many different built-in SAS formats that you can use, and you can also create your own. I will list a few of the most popular SAS formats here, but you will definitely want to make note of the ones that you use most frequently in your work.

- If you are dealing with very large numbers, you might want to use the *COMMAw.d* format to display commas in your numeric results.
- If you are working with currency values, you can use the *DOLLARw.d* format to display the dollar sign in front of your values.
- *PERCENTw.d* displays values as a percentage.
- The *Zw.d* format adds leading zeros to a number until the number reaches the specified width.
- *MMDDYYw.* is the most common date format I come across, though you might need to put a date in *DDMMYYw.* format or *YYMMDDw.* format.

To apply a format to a variable, add a FORMAT statement to your DATA step, specify the variable name that you want to apply it to, and then the format that you would like to use. Don't forget the period! You can assign multiple formats with a single FORMAT statement.

Continuing with the data set from the Manipulating Values section, let's add some formats[12] to these variables to see how they are displayed differently. Table 29 displays the results.

```
data Format;
     set input.Donations_JUL;
     format DOB mmddyy8. Donation_Date YYMMDD10.
     Donation dollar10.2 First_Name $1.
     Merchandise best8. Last_Name $upcase15.;
run;
```

Table 29: Formatted Donations_Jul Data Set

First_ Name	Last_ Name	Address	DOB	Donation	Donation_ Date	Merchandise
J	BROWN	6523 E Cherry St	05/22/57	$500.00	2022-07-12	122.68
K	GREEN	3111 Orange Ave	03/16/89	$25.00	2022-07-13	57.23
S	HOLMES	221B Baker Street	01/06/77	$221.00	2022-07-08	0

Note: Informats are identical to formats except they are typically used to tell SAS how to import/read data, whereas formats tell SAS how to display/output data.

6.6.1 User-Defined Formats

While SAS has several built-in formats to choose from, users often find that they need to create a specific format for their data to meet their business needs. Maybe you have custom categories for how Age should be grouped in your data for reporting purposes. Or perhaps you would like SAS to display each of your numeric values representing race or gender in words. Whatever your needs, you can easily create a format that works for you. To create a format, use the following syntax:

```
proc format;
     VALUE format-name
     Data-value-1 = 'Label 1'
     Data-value-2 = 'Label 2';
run;
```

---

[12] The BEST *w.* format writes as many significant digits as possible for each value in the width specified. Sometimes scientific notation is used to retain information that would otherwise be cut off. Formats only impact how the data is displayed, they do not change the actual value stored in SAS.

The PROC FORMAT statement tells SAS that you are defining one or more formats. The second statement starts with the VALUE keyword followed by the name of the format that you are creating. Your format name should start with a letter or underscore, not end in a number, not be longer than 32 characters, and not be the same as a format supplied by SAS. If you are applying the format to a character variable, you will need to add a $ in front of the format name.

Next, provide the labels that you would like to apply to the values of a variable in your data set. The original variable values are found on the left side of the equal sign, and the associated formatted values are on the right side. Add a semicolon after your last label, and then add the RUN statement.

Consider the following data set representing the fictional results of five people surveyed about their self-rated health (Table 30). We want to print the data in a more user-friendly format so that people will better understand what the data means. The following formats are applied to help clarify the results.

Table 30: Survey Data Set

Participant	Gender	Income	Health
1	M	20,000	2
2	F	78,000	4
3	M	105,000	5
4	X	55,000	3
5	F	42,000	1

Example 1: Add text format to the numeric values of a variable

```
proc format;
    VALUE HEALTH_TXT
          1   = "Poor"
          2   = "Fair"
          3   = "Good"
          4   = "Very Good"
          5   = "Excellent";
run;
```

Example 2: Add text format to a range of numeric values of a variable

```
proc format;
    VALUE INCOME_TXT
    LOW - < 25000 = "Low"
    25000 - < 75000 = "Middle"
    75000 - HIGH   = "High";
run;
```

Example 3: Add text format to character values of a variable

```
proc format;
    VALUE $GENDER_TXT
            "M"   = "Male"
            "F"   = "Female"
            OTHER = "Other";
run;
```

While the examples above are broken into three PROC FORMAT steps, it is possible to define more than one format in a single PROC FORMAT step. You will need to add multiple VALUE statements and always add a semicolon after the final label in each individual format.

Now that the formats have been defined, we can assign these formats as a property of our Survey variables using a FORMAT statement in the DATA step.

```
data Survey_Formatted;
    SET input.Survey;
        FORMAT Health HEALTH_TXT. Income INCOME_TXT. Gender $GENDER_TXT.;
run;
proc print data=Survey_Formatted; run;
```

Any results will now print with the formatted values rather than the underlying data values (Table 31).

Table 31: Formatted Survey Data Set

Obs	Participant	Gender	Income	Health
1	1	Male	Low	Fair
2	2	Female	High	Very Good
3	3	Male	High	Excellent
4	4	Other	Middle	Good
5	5	Female	Middle	Poor

If you assign a format using the FORMAT statement in a PROC step, that format will be assigned to results of the procedure but will not be applied to the underlying data or future DATA or PROC steps unless reassigned.

6.6.2 Storing User-Defined Formats

All formats are stored in catalogs. When you create a user-defined format, that format is saved to the Formats catalog in the WORK library. The format will exist for the duration of your SAS session but will be deleted when the session ends. Therefore, every time you start a new session, you will need to run the PROC FORMAT statement for SAS to be able to properly reassign the format(s) to your data.

To ensure this is not an issue, many people move their PROC FORMAT statements to the beginning of the program that uses these formats. That way, when the program is run in full, the formats are defined at the beginning of the program and can be used/applied throughout the rest of the program.

However, some people use user-defined formats in several of their programs, and do not want to copy and paste these formats to the beginning of every single program that uses them. There are a few options here.

My favorite option is to add your user-defined formats to your autoexec file. An autoexec file is a program that runs every single time that you open SAS. You want to add things here that you use frequently and need throughout your programs. For example, many people add macros or library assignments to their autoexec file to not have to rerun this code for each individual program. However, you want to avoid burdening your autoexec file with a lot of SAS code. If you read in data sets/perform calculations here, SAS will take forever to start up because it automatically runs everything in the autoexec file before you can even start coding. So, save the autoexec for quick things like system options and assigning frequently used formats, macros, and LIBNAMES. Editing your autoexec file can differ depending on what version of SAS you use. You can find it under **Options > Autoexec file** in SAS Studio® V. In SAS® Enterprise Guide®, you can go to **Options > SAS Programs**, check the box next to **Submit SAS code when server is connected**, click **Edit…**, and add the code that you want SAS to run when it connects to the server.

If you have several formats/code snippets that you want SAS to run that you use in many programs, but you don't want SAS to automatically run them every time it opens, you can use something called a global statement. For this option, you create a program that defines your formats, sets your macros, and can even perform common cleaning or analysis steps on your data sets. Instead of copying this code into several of your programs, you can simply save this code as a single program, and then tell SAS to run this program when you are coding in a different program. Super cool! You can do this by using the global statement %INCLUDE. Let's say you create your user-defined formats program called formats.sas and save it to the following location: C:\Documents\SAS\frequent\formats.sas. Now, when you open a new program, you can add a statement at the top that says:

```
%INCLUDE "C:\Documents\SAS\frequent\formats.sas";
```

SAS will find this program and run it in its entirety. Everything in that program has now been defined and is in your WORK library. You can continue coding and use any formats defined in your formats program.

Finally, you can create your own permanent format catalog. First, use a LIBNAME statement to define the location where you want your formats saved.

```
LIBNAME PERM 'C:\SASPermFiles'
```

Next, when creating your user-defined formats, define the catalog location and name in your PROC FORMAT statement to tell SAS where to permanently save your formats. In this example, the catalog is called Formats, and the location is the same as the PERM LIBREF (C:\SASPermFiles).

```
proc format LIBRARY=PERM.Formats;
     <user defined format code>;
run;
```

Now, you must tell SAS where your format catalog(s) are located and in what order to search for them.

```
OPTIONS FMTSEARCH = (PERM.FORMATS);
```

SAS now knows to search the Formats catalog in the PERM library whenever formats are applied to variables in the rest of the SAS program.

7 Combining and Aggregating Data

There are many different ways to combine (merge) data in SAS. Before digging into this section, make sure you have read and understand the Sorting and De-duplicating Data section above. I cannot stress enough the importance of understanding what variable(s) your data is unique by. You will also need to understand what key fields are required for matching data and how you want to join your data.

It is important to understand conceptually what you want out of your data merge before you even attempt to start coding. When combining data, I always ask myself the following questions:

1. What are each of my data sets unique by, and do I need to de-duplicate the data before combining?
2. What variables from each data set (if any) am I using to link these data sets together? In other words, are there key fields I am matching on?
3. What variables from each data set do I want in the final data set?
4. What rows do I want to be returned after the merge? Rows that were included in the first data set only (with information from data set 2 added), rows that were in the second data set only (with information from data set 1 added), only the rows that were in both data sets, or all rows that were in either data set?

These answers tell me the best way to go about combining the data.

7.1 Combing Data Using the DATA Step

7.1.1 Appending Data

This simplest case of combining data from two or more tables is when you need to append (or stack) data from two or more tables together into one table. Sometimes, you have two tables with the same variables but different records/rows that must be combined into one table. This often happens with data that is collected over time. The following two tables represent received donations, but one was collected in July (Table 32), whereas the other was collected in August (Table 33).

Table 32: Donations_JUL Data Set

First_ Name	Last_ Name	Address	DOB	Donation	Donation_ Date	Merchandise
John	Brown	6523 E Cherry St	5/22/1957	$500	7/12/2022	$122.68
Kelsey	Green	3111 Orange Ave	3/16/1989	$25	7/13/2022	$57.23
Sherlock	Holmes	221B Baker Street	1/6/1977	$221	7/8/2022	$0.00

Table 33: Donations_AUG Data Set

First_ Name	Last_ Name	Address	DOB	Donation	Donation_ Date	Merchandise
John	Brown	6523 E Cherry St	5/22/1957	$250	8/12/2022	$59.82
Kelsey	Green	3111 Orange Ave	3/16/1989	$50	8/13/2022	$102.13
Sherlock	Holmes	221B Baker Street	1/6/1977	$221	8/8/2022	$0.00

Essentially, all we want to do here is stack these two tables on top of each other so that all the donation data is in one table with six rows rather than in two tables with three rows each. Each row is unique, so we do not need to de-duplicate or merge the two data sets together on an ID field to pull in additional columns. Instead, we want all rows and all columns from both data sets. To do this, put both data set names in a single SET statement.

```
data Donations_All;
    set input.Donations_JUL input.Donations_AUG;
run;
```

Table 34: Appending Data – Donations_All Data Set

First_ Name	Last_ Name	Address	DOB	Donation	Donation_ Date	Merchandise
John	Brown	6523 E Cherry St	5/22/1957	$500	7/12/2022	$122.68
Kelsey	Green	3111 Orange Ave	3/16/1989	$25	7/13/2022	$57.23
Sherlock	Holmes	221B Baker Street	1/6/1977	$221	7/8/2022	$0.00
John	Brown	6523 E Cherry St	5/22/1957	$250	8/12/2022	$59.82
Kelsey	Green	3111 Orange Ave	3/16/1989	$50	8/13/2022	$102.13
Sherlock	Holmes	221B Baker Street	1/6/1977	$221	8/8/2022	$0.00

Now, we have a single data set called Donations_All with all rows from Donations_JUL and Donations_AUG stacked on top of each other (Table 34). You can list all of the data sets you want to stack in the SET statement.

PROC APPEND also enables you to stack data sets, but rather than creating a new data set with all of the combined data, it overwrites and updates the original base table to contain all of the records. The APPEND procedure is more efficient when the base data set is large.

7.1.2 One-to-One Merge

The next type of DATA step merge is called a one-to-one merge. A one-to-one merge means that the ID that you are matching your data sets on is unique in each data set. In other words, each ID value only has one row in data set 1 and one row in data set 2. This merge is useful when you have two data sets with the same unique id field(s), and you need to add additional information (columns) to one of the tables.

The basic syntax for a DATA step merge is below.

```
data output-table-name;
    merge input-table-name1 input-table-name2;
     by column(s);
run;
```

When merging data using the MERGE statement, you must ensure that the variables that you are joining on (also known as the BY variables) between two (or more) data sets have the same name and data type, and that the data sets are all sorted by the variable(s) that you are merging on.

If a variable name exists on both data sets, the column in the first data set will be overwritten with the values in the second data set in the output table. This is fine for the BY variables that you are matching on but could have unintended consequences for any variables you are not matching on.

For example, let's say we want to merge the Donations_JUL and Donations_AUG data sets. We want the output table to have three rows (one for each donor) and include the Donation column for the July data set and the Donation column for the August data set. Without renaming at least one of the Donation columns when merging, this data would result in the second data set's Donation value overwriting the first data set's Donation value (Table 35).

```
proc sort data=input.Donations_JUL out=Sort_JUL;
by First_Name Last_Name DOB; run;
proc sort data=input.Donations_AUG out=Sort_AUG;
by First_Name Last_Name DOB; run;
data Donations_Merged ;
    merge Sort_JUL Sort_AUG ;
    by First_Name Last_Name DOB;
run;
```

Table 35: Bad DATA Step Merge

First_Name	Last_Name	Address	DOB	Donation	Donation_Date	Merchandise
John	Brown	6523 E Cherry St	05/22/1957	$250	08/12/2022	$59.82
Kelsey	Green	3111 Orange Ave	03/16/1989	$50	08/13/2022	$102.13
Sherlock	Holmes	221B Baker Street	01/06/1977	$221	08/08/2022	$0.00

Since all of the column names in the first data set (Donations_JUL) are the same as the column names in the second data set (Donations_AUG), the columns in Donations_AUG overwrite all of the columns in Donations_JUL. This is not the output that we are looking for. We want one Donation column from the July data set and the other Donation column from the August data set to show up together in the final output table. To do this, let's rename and relabel the Donation columns and drop the information that we do not need (Table 36).

```
proc sort data=input.Donations_JUL out=Sort_JUL;
by First_Name Last_Name DOB; run;
proc sort data=input.Donations_AUG out=Sort_AUG;
by First_Name Last_Name DOB; run;
data Donations_Merged (drop=Donation_Date Merchandise);
    merge Sort_JUL (rename=(Donation=Donation_JUL))
            Sort_AUG (rename=(Donation=Donation_AUG)) ;
    by First_Name Last_Name DOB;
    label Donation_JUL='July Donations' Donation_AUG='August
    Donations';
run;
```

Table 36: Donations_Merged Data Set

First_Name	Last_Name	Address	DOB	Donation_JUL	Donation_AUG
John	Brown	6523 E Cherry St	05/22/1957	$500	$250
Kelsey	Green	3111 Orange Ave	03/16/1989	$25	$50
Sherlock	Holmes	221B Baker Street	01/06/1977	$221	$221

That's better. Since we renamed the Donations column in the Donations_JUL data set to Donations_JUL, the renamed Donations_AUG column did not overwrite it because it had a different name.

7.1.3 One-to-Many Merge

The most complex DATA step merge is called the one-to-many merge (or many-to-one). This means that on one data set, there are many rows with the same ID value that you are merging on, while the other data set has only one row for each ID value.

For example, let's say you have a data set called Claim that contains patient claim data (Table 37). Your data set is unique by the ClaimID field. This means that the same patient (PatientID) might appear in multiple rows if they have more than one claim. The ClaimID column, however, is unique as each value is never repeated on any other row. The data set also has a variable called Date, representing the date of the claim, and Ctype, a numeric field with a number from 1 to 900, representing the type of procedure the patient received. Looking only at this data set, it is impossible to know what these procedures are as they are only represented as numeric codes.

Table 37: Claim Data Set

PatientID	ClaimID	Date	Ctype
221923797	21460513062	755	05/17/2022
567660147	80995718432	177	11/12/2021
567660147	86902627542	222	11/12/2021
774658165	91833838898	755	05/28/2021
811279234	39343015857	177	09/05/2021
811279234	75217985959	300	12/09/2021
811279234	50564174591	496	03/31/2022
935472958	90557924941	562	10/31/2020
935472958	62369319156	41	02/18/2021

Let's say you have another data set called Claim_Type containing one variable called Ctype and one called Claim_Desc (Table 38). This table is unique by Ctype and lists the numbers 1-900 with their associated claim description in the Claim_Desc field. Rather than showing all 900 rows, the example data set below highlights a few selected rows to illustrate the merge process.

Table 38: Claim_Type Data Set

Ctype	Claim_Desc
41	Annual Physical Exam
177	Physical Therapy
222	X-Ray Shoulder
300	MRI Spine
496	X-Ray Femur
562	Lipid Panel
755	Flu Vaccine

Now that you have a separate data set that tells you what each Ctype value represents, you want to merge the Claim_Desc column from the Claim_Type data set onto your Claim data set so that you actually know what all of the Ctype codes mean. In this scenario, you would want to merge the two data sets on the Ctype variable and pull in the Claim_Desc field from the Claim_Type data set (Table 39).

```
proc sort data=input.Claim out=sort_claim; by Ctype; run;
proc sort data=input.Claim_Type out=sort_claim_type; by Ctype; run;
data Merged_Claims;
    merge sort_claim sort_claim_type;
    by Ctype;
proc sort; by PatientID Date;
run;
```

Table 39: Merged Claims

PatientID	ClaimID	Ctype	Date	Claim_Desc
221923797	21460513062	755	05/17/2022	Flu Vaccine
567660147	80995718432	177	11/12/2021	Physical Therapy
567660147	86902627542	222	11/12/2021	X-Ray Shoulder
774658165	91833838898	755	05/28/2021	Flu Vaccine
811279234	39343015857	177	09/05/2021	Physical Therapy
811279234	75217985959	300	12/09/2021	MRI Spine
811279234	50564174591	496	03/31/2022	X-Ray Femur
935472958	90557924941	562	10/31/2020	Lipid Panel
935472958	62369319156	41	02/18/2021	Annual Physical Exam

7.2 PROC SQL

7.2.1 Types of Joins

The most complex part of merging data using PROC SQL is usually identifying the type of join you want. Before we get into the SAS syntax for PROC SQL, let's walk through a conceptual example of each of the four joins: left join, right join, inner join, and full join. The tables below represent two data sets that we want to join (Table 40).

Table 40: Jobs and Salaries Data Sets

Data Set 1: Jobs		Data Set 2: Salaries	
Name	Job	Name	Salary
Ashley	Teller	Emma	$100,000
Emma	Manager	John	$55,000
John	Accountant	Susan	$40,000

7.2.1.1 Left Join

Let's say your HR representative wants to see a list of each employee that has a job title (all rows in data set 1) with their associated salary information appended on when available. To get this list, you would left join the Jobs and Salaries data sets matching on employee Name. A left join returns all rows in data set 1 (Jobs) and appends on any requested information from data set 2 (Salaries) when available. This would result in the following table (Table 41).

Table 41: Left Join of Jobs and Salaries Data Sets

| Name | Left Joined Data | |
	Job	Salary
Ashley	Teller	.
Emma	Manager	$100,000
John	Accountant	$55,000

Notice that Ashley still appears in the data set using a left join because a record for her did exist in data set 1 even though there was no associated record for her in data set 2. Since she was not in the Salaries data set, a salary was not found for her. Therefore, she is assigned a Salary value of missing. As a reminder from the Values section, missing numeric values are represented by a period in SAS.

7.2.1.2 Right Join

Alternatively, the HR representative might want a report of all known employees with salaries at the bank (all rows in data set 2) with job titles appended, when available. To get this list, you would right join the Jobs and Salaries data sets on employee Name. This will return all rows in data set 2 and add information from data set 1 when available. The results look like this (Table 42).

Table 42: Right Join of Jobs and Salaries Data Sets

| Name | Right Joined Data | |
	Salary	Job
Emma	$100,000	Manager
John	$55,000	Accountant
Susan	$40,000	

When using a right join, Ashley no longer appears in the merged data set (because she does not have Salary information), but Susan does. Since Susan is not in data set 1, however, the Job field is blank/missing for her in the merged data set. As a reminder, missing character variables are represented by a space in SAS.

7.2.1.3 Inner Join

Your HR manager might want only the list of employees with a known job title and salary. In this case, you would inner join the Jobs data set with the Salaries data set on Name. This will return only the records on data set 1 that also existed in data set 2 (Table 43).

Table 43: Inner Join of Jobs and Salaries Data Sets

Inner Joined Data		
Name	**Job**	**Salary**
Emma	Manager	$100,000
John	Accountant	$55,000

Only Emma and John had both Job and Salary information. Ashley and Susan were dropped from the merged data set since they were not in both input data sets.

7.2.1.4 Full Join

Finally, your HR representative might want to know all available information so that he can work on filling in any missing data. In this case, you should do a full join on Name so that all rows from data set 1 and all rows from data set 2 are included (Table 44).

Table 44: Full Join of Jobs and Salaries Data Sets

Full Joined Data		
Name	**Job**	**Salary**
Ashley	Teller	.
Emma	Manager	$100,000
John	Accountant	$55,000
Susan		$40,000

All employees are included in the merged data set and have missing values where they did not have a Name match on the other data set.

Before you start coding, always walk through what is needed conceptually and what type of join you need to achieve the desired result. As data analysts, we often get requests to merge data with little instruction on how to join it and what the resulting data will be used for. Don't be afraid to ask about the goals/purpose of the merged data set to make sure you provide the most useful information.

For example, suppose a client asks you to merge the jobs and salaries data. In this case, they likely will not understand the question if you ask them what kind of join you should do. But you could ask whether they want all employee information, even if there is missing information, or whether they only want data for employees with both job and salary information.

7.2.2 PROC SQL Syntax

My preferred method for merging data in SAS is PROC SQL, which enables you to pick and choose what variables you want from data sets. Sorting is not necessary, and the variables that you are matching on are not required to have the same name. A PROC SQL step is structured differently than a DATA step and ends with a QUIT statement rather than a RUN statement. Since there is a lot of flexibility in which variables you can pull in, it is good practice to specify which data set you are referring to when referencing a particular variable. For example, if both data sets have a variable named Income, you will need to specify if you want SAS to select the Income variable from data set 1 or the Income variable from data set 2. PROC SQL enables you to nickname each table so that you do not have to write the full name of the table out every time you reference a variable from that table. To nickname a table, enter the table name in the FROM clause and then type AS and the name that you want to nickname the table. I typically nickname my first table a, my second table b, and so on. I use a one-letter nickname for efficiency. But you can nickname your tables whatever you like, as long as it follows SAS naming conventions.

```
proc sql;
    CREATE TABLE output-table-name AS
    SELECT column(s)
    FROM input-table-name AS nickname
    <join type input-table-name2 AS nickname2>
    ON column(s)
    WHERE expression
    GROUP BY column(s)
    HAVING expression
    ORDER BY column(s);
quit;
```

In a typical PROC SQL step, you start with a **CREATE TABLE** statement that names the output table that you are creating. If you leave this statement out, SAS will print the table results to the results viewer rather than create a table in the WORK library. This can be problematic when dealing with large data sets.

The **SELECT** statement tells SAS which variables you want to pull from one or more tables. Since you can pull variables from multiple tables simultaneously, you must start with the table name, add a period, and then the variable name. Alternatively, you can use the table nickname, period, and variable name denotation (i.e., SELECT student.student_ID or SELECT a.student_ID). If you want to name the variable something different or are calculating a variable, you will use the AS keyword to name the variable (i.e., a.StudentID as ID or max(a.score) as max_score).

The **FROM** clause tells SAS what input tables you want to read in and specifies the join criteria (left, right, inner, full) when merging tables. You can nickname your tables with the AS keyword to use shorthand when referencing any variables from that table throughout your PROC SQL step.

The **ON** clause provides the name of the variable(s) that the data sets are being matched on.

The **WHERE** clause tells SAS if you want to apply a filter to the records that you are reading in from the input table(s). Be sure to specify the table or table nickname if you filter on particular variables (i.e., WHERE a.year=2002 and b.contribution>25).

The **GROUP BY** clause enables you to aggregate and group your data by one or more specified variables. For example, if you have a table with 10 exam records for each student, a GROUP BY clause would enable you to output one record for each student with their average test score. See the PROC SQL GROUP BY Example section below for more details.

Like the WHERE clause, the **HAVING** clause is also a way to filter rows. But rather than filtering rows out of the input tables, the HAVING clause reads in all rows from the input tables but filters out rows that do not meet specific criteria before writing it out to the output table.

The **ORDER BY** clause is the same as a SORT procedure. It tells SAS which variables to sort the output table by.

7.2.2.1 PROC SQL Data Merge Example

Let's say you have a data set called Student_Demographic, and you want to merge on all exam info for those students from a file called Assessment. The Student_Demographic table has the following variables: StudentID, Race, Gender, and Age (Table 45). This file is unique by StudentID.

Table 45: Student_Demographic Data Set

StudentID	Race	Gender	Age
MU100256	Black	Female	21
SG547868	White	Female	19
FR364701	Hispanic	Male	21
GR259262	White	Male	20

The Assessment file has the following variables: StudentID, Exam_Date, Subject, Score (Table 46). StudentID is not unique in this file as a student might have multiple test scores. This file is unique by the combination of StudentID and Subject since each student has one test score in each subject.

Table 46: Assessment Data Set

StudentID	Exam_Date	Subject	Score
MU100256	11/22/2019	ELA	90
MU100256	3/19/2019	MATH	82
MU100256	5/20/2019	SCIENCE	98
SG547868	11/22/2019	ELA	74
SG547868	3/19/2019	MATH	68
SG547868	5/20/2019	SCIENCE	
FR364701	11/22/2019	ELA	88
FR364701	3/19/2019	MATH	100
FR364701	5/20/2019	SCIENCE	97
KR159435	11/22/2019	ELA	50
KR159435	3/19/2019	MATH	66
KR159435	5/20/2019	SCIENCE	0

To match these data sets together, you would use the StudentID field. This is a one-to-many merge since StudentID is unique in the demographic table but repeats in the assessment file. If you want to only keep records for students with both a demographic record and an assessment record (inner join), the code would be:

```
proc sql;
    create table Demo_Exam as
    select a.StudentID, a.Race, a.Gender, b.Exam_Date,
    b.Subject, b.Score
    from input.Student_Demographic as a
    inner join input.Assessment as b
    on a.StudentID=b.StudentID;
quit;
```

The resulting table contains records for only the students that existed on both files (Table 47). Adding a HAVING clause of Score > . would remove the observation below with a missing assessment score (StudentID= SG547868).

Table 47: Demo_Exam Data Set (Inner Join)

StudentID	Race	Gender	Exam_Date	Subject	Score
MU100256	Black	Female	11/22/2019	ELA	90
MU100256	Black	Female	03/19/2019	MATH	82
MU100256	Black	Female	05/20/2019	SCIENCE	98
SG547868	White	Female	11/22/2019	ELA	74
SG547868	White	Female	03/19/2019	MATH	68
SG547868	White	Female	05/20/2019	SCIENCE	
FR364701	Hispanic	Male	11/22/2019	ELA	88
FR364701	Hispanic	Male	03/19/2019	MATH	100
FR364701	Hispanic	Male	05/20/2019	SCIENCE	97

Suppose you want to keep all records on the Student_Demographic file regardless of whether they have a corresponding Assessment record. In that case, you'd use a left join rather than an inner join. If you want all Assessment records regardless of whether they have a Student_Demographic record, you'd do a right join. Finally, if you want all records on either file, you'd do a full join rather than an inner join.

```
proc sql;
    create table Demo_Exam as
    select coalesce(a.StudentID, b.StudentID) as student_ID,
    a.Race, a.Gender, b.Exam_Date, b.Subject, b.Score
    from input.Student_Demographic as a
    full join input.Assessment as b
    on a.StudentID=b.StudentID;
quit;
```

A cool trick if you are doing a full join and your matching ID (in this case StudentID) in some cases is populated on data set 1 with no corresponding record on the data set 2 (e.g., StudentID="GR259262") while in other cases is populated on data set 2 with no corresponding record on data set 1 (e.g., StudentID="KR159435"), you can use the COALESCE function.

In your SELECT statement, enter: COALESCE(a.StudentID, b.StudentID) as StudentID. This creates a new variable called StudentID that is filled in with the Student_Demographic StudentID when it exists but uses the Assessment StudentID if the StudentID does not exist/is missing on the Student_Demographic file. If you only used the StudentID from the demographic file (select a.StudentID), the table below would have missing values for StudentID "KR159435". If you only used the StudentID from the assessment file (SELECT b.StudentID), the table below would have a missing value for student ID "GR259262" as this ID does not exist on the Assessment file. COALESCE allows us to pull in all StudentID information available (Table 48).

Table 48: Demo_Exam Data Set (Full Join)

StudentID	Race	Gender	Exam_Date	Subject	Score
FR364701	Hispanic	Male	11/22/2019	ELA	88
FR364701	Hispanic	Male	05/20/2019	SCIENCE	97
FR364701	Hispanic	Male	03/19/2019	MATH	100
GR259262	White	Male			
KR159435			03/19/2019	MATH	66
KR159435			11/22/2019	ELA	50
KR159435			05/20/2019	SCIENCE	0
MU100256	Black	Female	05/20/2019	SCIENCE	98
MU100256	Black	Female	11/22/2019	ELA	90
MU100256	Black	Female	03/19/2019	MATH	82
SG547868	White	Female	05/20/2019	SCIENCE	
SG547868	White	Female	03/19/2019	MATH	68
SG547868	White	Female	11/22/2019	ELA	74

You can also use the COALESCE function on other variables (that are not the matching ID). Remember, the first variable you list in the function takes precedence, and the second specified variable only fills in information missing from the first variable. If you add a third variable to the function, it will only fill in information missing in both the first and second variables, and so on.

Another shortcut available in PROC SQL is the * symbol. If you want to select all variables from the Student_Demographic table, you'd enter: SELECT a.*. To select all variables from the Assessment table, type SELECT b.*. If you want all variables from both tables, you'd simply enter * for the SELECT statement.

```
proc sql;
    create table Demo_Exam as
    select *
    from input.Student_Demographic as a
    full join input.Assessment(rename=(StudentID=ID)) as b
    on a.StudentID=b.ID;
quit;
```

If you tell SAS to pull in all variables from both data sets, but both data sets have a variable with the same name (like StudentID), SAS will give you a warning message because it does not know which StudentID column you want. You can get around this by renaming the duplicate variable name on one of the data sets. Be sure to update your ON clause accordingly if you change the name of a match ID variable, like StudentID (Table 49).

Table 49: Demo_Exam Data Set (RENAME Option)

StudentID	Race	Gender	Age	ID	Exam_Date	Subject	Score
FR364701	Hispanic	Male	21	FR364701	11/22/2019	ELA	88
FR364701	Hispanic	Male	21	FR364701	05/20/2019	SCIENCE	97
FR364701	Hispanic	Male	21	FR364701	03/19/2019	MATH	100
GR259262	White	Male	20				
				KR159435	03/19/2019	MATH	66
				KR159435	11/22/2019	ELA	50
				KR159435	05/20/2019	SCIENCE	0
MU100256	Black	Female	21	MU100256	05/20/2019	SCIENCE	98
MU100256	Black	Female	21	MU100256	11/22/2019	ELA	90
MU100256	Black	Female	21	MU100256	03/19/2019	MATH	82
SG547868	White	Female	19	SG547868	05/20/2019	SCIENCE	
SG547868	White	Female	19	SG547868	03/19/2019	MATH	68
SG547868	White	Female	19	SG547868	11/22/2019	ELA	74

7.2.2.2 PROC SQL GROUP BY Example

The GROUP BY clause is great for aggregating data. This is useful when you want to add, count, or take the minimum/maximum of all values down a particular column for a specified group. Unlike the calculations that we saw in the Data Transformations section that calculate values across a row, the GROUP BY clause makes it possible to make calculations down a column. This restructures your output data so that you have fewer rows than your input table that is unique by whatever variable(s) you identified in your GROUP BY clause.

For example, let's say you want to get the average assessment score for each student in the Assessment data set across all three subjects. To do this, you would tell SAS to select the StudentID variable, take the Score variable's average, and group the results by StudentID. You can sort by descending average Score to rank the students from highest to lowest performing.

```
proc sql;
    create table Avg_Assessment as
    select StudentID, avg(Score) as Avg_Score
    from input.Assessment
    group by StudentID
    order by Avg_Score desc;
quit;
```

The code above produces a data set called Avg_Assessment with two columns: StudentID and Avg_Score (Table 50). Each student will have one row in the data set, displaying that student's average test score across all three subjects. Notice that one student, "SG547868," has a missing test score for "SCIENCE". The average function takes the average of available data, "MATH" and "ELA" and provides an average score of (68+74)/2=71.

Table 50: Avg_Assessment Data Set Using GROUP BY Clause

StudentID	Avg_Score
FR364701	95
MU100256	90
SG547868	71
KR159435	38.66666667

One error that is easy to get when attempting a GROUP BY aggregation is that you add a variable to your SELECT statement that is not one of the GROUP BY variables and you do not tell SAS to do some kind of aggregation function with it. For example, if you added the Exam_Date variable to the SELECT statement in the example above, SAS would be unable to GROUP BY the StudentID as it does not know which date to select for each student. This yields undesirable results (Table 51).

Table 51: GROUP BY Error

StudentID	Exam_Date	Avg_Score
FR364701	11/22/2019	95
FR364701	03/19/2019	95
FR364701	05/20/2019	95
MU100256	05/20/2019	90
MU100256	03/19/2019	90
MU100256	11/22/2019	90
SG547868	11/22/2019	71
SG547868	03/19/2019	71
SG547868	05/20/2019	71
KR159435	05/20/2019	38.66666667
KR159435	11/22/2019	38.66666667
KR159435	03/19/2019	38.66666667

To fix this issue, make sure that some calculation is performed on every variable in your SELECT statement except for the GROUP BY variable(s). This is true even for character variables that have the same value populated for all rows of the BY group (e.g., Race). Tell SAS to take the max value of that variable, and the GROUP BY clause will work. It will only keep one instance of the value in the output data set. In this example, add the MAX function to pull only the last exam date, and then the GROUP BY clause will work (Table 52).

```
proc sql;
      create table Avg_Assessment as
      select StudentID,
      max(Exam_Date) as Last_Exam format=mmddyy10.,
      avg(Score) as Avg_Score
      from input.Assessment
      group by StudentID
      order by Avg_Score desc;
quit;
```

Since you are creating a new variable called Last_Exam by taking the maximum date value, make sure to tell SAS how to format the new date or it will display the integer date value instead.

Table 52: GROUP BY with Max Exam Date

StudentID	Last_Exam	Avg_Score
FR364701	11/22/2019	95
MU100256	11/22/2019	90
SG547868	11/22/2019	71
KR159435	11/22/2019	38.66666667

8 Comparing Data

Now that we've covered how data is merged, we can discuss how to compare data sets. When you are just getting started with coding, it is helpful to practice by trying to replicate projects that others have already done. This way, you can write your code and compare your output table to the actual output table to see if you get the same results. If you see any differences, this can help you identify areas to work on and ask follow-up questions about. Also, if you are working on a high-stakes or high-visibility project, you might be tasked with replicating work with one or more people for quality assurance before the results are published.

Finally, as your data analysis skills grow, you will inevitably look back at some of your beginning programs and cringe at how clunky they are. You will likely want to go back and make your programs more streamlined and efficient. It is helpful to run your new code against your old code to make sure that your new code is still producing the same results. These are all examples of why comparing data is such a useful skill to have in your toolbox.

8.1 DATA Step Compare Merge

One way to compare data is by using a DATA step merge. This is extremely helpful when you are trying to compare two data sets and want to create three output tables: records that appear in both tables (Both), records that appear in data set 1 only (Base_Only), and records that appear in data set 2 only (Compare_Only). Make sure you sort your Base and Compare tables by the ID(s) that you want to merge on first. Once the tables are sorted, run the code below to get the three output tables. Update the BY statement to reflect the variables that you are merging on and the Base and Compare table names in the MERGE statement to your two input table names.

```
data Base_Only Compare_Only Both;
    merge Base (in=a) Compare (in=b);
    by ID;
    if a=1 and b=0 then output Base_Only;
    if b=1 and a=0 then output Compare_Only;
    if a=1 and b=1 then output Both;
run;
```

Note that this merge only looks at the variables that you are merging on (the BY variables) to see whether a record is in both data sets or only in a single data set. It does not compare other fields in your data set. So, if you have a record with the same ID on both data sets, but the Name field on data set 1 is different than the Name field on data set 2, the merge above will list the record in the Both data set and keep only the Name from data set 2. To compare ***all fields*** in a data set, it is best to use <u>PROC COMPARE</u>.

8.2 PROC COMPARE

To compare two data sets on all fields, run a PROC COMPARE. Make sure you sort the two data sets by their unique ID(s). SAS compares row 1 of data set 1 to row 1 of data set 2, and so on. So, if your data isn't sorted properly, all rows will be marked as mismatches. Also, check to see whether both data sets have the same number of total records. If they do not, start with the <u>DATA Step Compare Merge</u> to discover what record(s) are missing in one of your data sets and whether they should be included. Once you have the same number of records and your data is properly sorted, you're ready to run the PROC COMPARE.

```
proc compare base=dataset1 compare=dataset2 out=nonmatches
    outnoequal outall listvar;
run;
```

In a COMPARE procedure, you will list the name of the first data set as the BASE= option and the name of the second data set as the COMPARE= option. These are the only two arguments required. However, you can include many different options to help visualize any differences. I included the options I find most useful above. You can output a data set of mismatches and specify the name for this table in the OUT= argument. The OUTNOEQUAL option tells SAS to only output records with at least one mismatched value for a row. The OUTALL option tells SAS to write one row for the Base data set followed by the same mismatched row in the Compare data set. It also writes rows that display what the difference/mismatched value is between the base and compare data sets as well as the percentage difference between the two values. LISTVAR is helpful if you want to see whether there is a column in one data set that does not exist in the other data set.

9 Reporting

As data analysts, we often view our job as accurately merging, cleaning/transforming, and analyzing data. But that is only half of the story. For all of your work to be effective and meaningful, you need to be able to communicate your results with others. Often, your audience is not made up of other data analysts, it is policy makers, communications directors, CEOs, or worse, the general public. If you try to copy and paste your output with ugly variable names like Amt_q1, I guarantee your audience's eyes will glaze over, and all your hard work will end up in the physical or digital recycle bin. As data analysts, we have a duty not only to analyze data but also to **_effectively communicate_** what that data says.

Luckily, SAS has several reporting options to help you communicate your results in an easy-to-understand way. PROC PRINT enables you to format and print information from SAS data tables to the Results tab. PROC REPORT enables you to create and format both detailed and summary reports. Finally, the output delivery system (ODS) allows for style and formatting enhancements to reports that can be output to different destinations like PDF or Microsoft Word.

9.1 PROC PRINT

PROC PRINT enables you to print all or selected portions from your output data tables. Frequently used options include:

- Adding titles and footnotes to the printed data table.
- Selecting certain variables or observations to print.
- Adding and displaying labels.
- Applying formats.

You can also change the font or size of the text in your table and apply background colors to specific rows, columns, or cells if the cell meets specified criteria (e.g., the cell is greater than 100 or the response was "yes").

In this example, we are printing data from the Donations_JUL data table. The NOOBS option means that the observation number (or row count) should not be included in the results. The LABEL option tells SAS to print the specified labels listed in the code below rather than the variable names as the column headers. The VAR statement lists the variable(s) that should be included in the report (and the order in which they should appear), and the LABEL statement defines the labels for each specified variable. A second VAR statement for the Donation variable specifies that this column should be displayed with a gold background. The FORMAT option is used to choose how the Donation_Date values are displayed. Finally, the SUM statement tells SAS to add up all values of the Donations variable and display the total, $746, in the report (Table 53).

```
proc print data=input.donations_JUL noobs label;
     var First_Name Last_Name Address Donation_Date;
     var Donation / style(data)={backgroundcolor=gold};
     label First_Name = 'Donor First Name'
           Last_Name = 'Donor Last Name'
           Donation_Date = 'Donation Date';
     format Donation_Date date9.;
     sum Donation;
run;
```

Table 53: PROC PRINT Example with Labels

Donor First Name	Donor Last Name	Address	Donation Date	Donation
John	Brown	6523 E Cherry St	12JUL2022	$500
Kelsey	Green	3111 Orange Ave	13JUL2022	$25
Sherlock	Holmes	221B Baker Street	08JUL2022	$221
				$746

In In the following example, a format is applied so that readers of the report can easily distinguish between low, medium, and high donations. The format is named *donorlevel*, and Donations under $75 are classified as rose, those between $75 and $250 are classified as yellow, and Donations that are $250 or higher are classified as BILG, for brilliant yellow-green. Instead of the VAR Donations statement having a background color of gold like the previous example, it is given a background color of the *donorlevel* format. This means that the donation column will have a background color based on the donation value in the cell. Also, this example adds a title to the printed output that reads "Large Donors for Follow-Up Marketing Campaign" (Table 54).

```
proc format;
     value donorlevel
     low-<75='rose'
     75-<250='yellow'
     250-high='BILG';
run;

title 'Large Donors for Follow Up Marketing Campaign';
proc print data=input.donations_JUL noobs label;
     var First_Name Last_Name Address Donation_Date;
     var Donation / style(data)={backgroundcolor=donorlevel.};
     label First_Name = 'Donor First Name'
           Last_Name = 'Donor Last Name'
           Donation_Date = 'Donation Date'
           Donation = 'Donation Level';
     format Donation_Date date9.;
run;
title;
```

Table 54: PROC PRINT Example with Conditional Style Format

Large Donors for Follow Up Marketing Campaign

Donor First Name	Donor Last Name	Address	Donation Date	Donation Level
John	Brown	6523 E Cherry St	12JUL2022	$500
Kelsey	Green	3111 Orange Ave	13JUL2022	$25
Sherlock	Holmes	221B Baker Street	08JUL2022	$221

Note: If you'd like to customize your background colors, you can go to: https://support.sas.com/content/dam/SAS/support/en/books/pro-template-made-easy-a-guide-for-sas-users/62007_Appendix.pdf to see what color options are available. To learn more about style attributes that you can apply to your reports, visit: https://go.documentation.sas.com/doc/en/pgmsascdc/9.4_3.5/odsug/p1pt77toue3iyun0z4l9gth5as9f.htm.

9.2 PROC REPORT

Like PROC PRINT, PROC REPORT can also be used to print data tables. However, PROC REPORT has additional functionality that allows users to create spanning headings and merge cells with repeating data. PROC REPORT can also output and format summary reports/statistics. The general syntax for PROC REPORT is as follows:

```
proc report DATA=input-table-name <option(s)>;
     COLUMN variable-1 < … variable-n>;
     DEFINE variable-1 / <options>;
     DEFINE variable-n / <options>;
     COMPUTE; ENDCOMP;
     BREAK;
     RBREAK;
run;
```

The statements in PROC REPORT are defined as follows:

- The **DATA** statement specifies which data table you want to use for your report.
- The **COLUMN** statement tells SAS which variables/columns to include in the report and prints them in the order listed.
- The **DEFINE** statement explains how to use and display each defined variable. Without this statement, the variable name, label, and format information defaults to what exists in the data set.
- The **COMPUTE** and **ENDCOMP** statements are used to perform any calculations needed for the report.

- The **RBREAK** statement produces a report summary row at the beginning or end of a report, whereas the **BREAK** statement creates a summary for each grouping specified in the report.

A basic example of PROC REPORT can be found below. A data set called Demo_Exam is read in, and the COLUMN statement specifies that the variables StudentID, Exam_Date, Race, Gender, Subject, and Score should all be included in the report. The DEFINE statement and DISPLAY option are used for specified variables to tell SAS to print the text in single quotation marks as the column heading in the report rather than using the variable name. For example, the report will print Exam Date rather than Exam_Date as the header for the column representing the date on which the student took the exam (Table 55). If an alternative heading is not specified using the DISPLAY option for a variable listed in the COLUMN statement, the SAS variable name will be used as the column header or the variable's pre-defined label (when the LABEL option is used).

```
proc report DATA=input.demo_exam;
    COLUMN StudentID exam_date Race Gender subject score;
    DEFINE StudentID / DISPLAY 'Student ID';
    DEFINE exam_date / DISPLAY 'Exam Date';
    DEFINE subject / DISPLAY 'Subject';
    DEFINE score / DISPLAY 'Exam Score';
run;
```

Table 55: PROC REPORT Example

Student ID	Exam Date	Race	Gender	Subject	Exam Score
MU100256	11/22/2019	Black	Female	ELA	90
MU100256	03/19/2019	Black	Female	MATH	82
MU100256	05/20/2019	Black	Female	SCIENCE	98
SG547868	11/22/2019	White	Female	ELA	74
SG547868	03/19/2019	White	Female	MATH	68
SG547868	05/20/2019	White	Female	SCIENCE	.
FR364701	11/22/2019	Hispanic	Male	ELA	88
FR364701	03/19/2019	Hispanic	Male	MATH	100
FR364701	05/20/2019	Hispanic	Male	SCIENCE	97

The next example shows how to create spanning report headers, sort data, and add summary information to reports. Using parentheses in the COLUMN statement with specified text enables you to create spanning headings.

As you can see, 'Student Exam Scores 2019' is inside the first set of parentheses, indicating a spanning header covering all variables and additional subheadings in the report. Next, a second set of parentheses tells SAS that 'Student Info' is a subheading spanning the StudentID, Race, and Gender variables. The third set of parentheses indicate that 'Exam Info' is another subheading spanning across the Exam_Date, Subject, and Score variables. The ORDER option in the DEFINE statements explains that the report should be organized first by descending (from Z to A) StudentID, then by ascending (from A to Z) Race and ascending Gender.

The SPANROWS option in the DATA statement merges cells with repeating data. So instead of listing out the StudentID "SG547868" three times, the report lists it only once, and the additional two cells are merged with the first cell to indicate that the first three exams listed all belong to the same student. Race and Gender data are also merged as each student's race and gender do not change across different observations.

Additional options can be used for numeric variables. For example, when grouping data, summarizing data, or calculating new columns, you can specify how numeric information should be aggregated. For instance, when Score is defined, the ANALYSIS option is used with the specified statistic mean. This ensures that the average, or mean, is given when Score data is grouped. The ANALYSIS option is only used with numeric data. The BREAK statement provides a summary row for each student that reports that student's average test score. The RBREAK option is at the report level, so it provides a summary row for average exam score across all students. Summary statistics are calculated based on the specified statistic for each numeric variable listed in the report (Table 56).

```
proc report DATA=input.demo_exam spanrows;
    COLUMN ('Student Exam Scores 2019' ('Student Info'
    StudentID Race Gender) ('Exam Info' exam_date subject score));
    DEFINE StudentID / ORDER descending 'Student ID';
    DEFINE Race / ORDER;
    DEFINE Gender / ORDER;
    DEFINE exam_date / DISPLAY 'Exam Date';
    DEFINE score / ANALYSIS mean 'Exam Score';
    BREAK after StudentID / summarize;
    RBREAK after / summarize;
run;
```

Table 56: PROC REPORT Example with Custom Headers

Student Exam Scores 2019					
Student Info			Exam Info		
Student ID	Race	Gender	Exam Date	Subject	Exam Score
SG547868	White	Female	11/22/2019	ELA	74
			03/19/2019	MATH	68
			05/20/2019	SCIENCE	.
SG547868					71
MU100256	Black	Female	11/22/2019	ELA	90
			03/19/2019	MATH	82
			05/20/2019	SCIENCE	98
MU100256					90
FR364701	Hispanic	Male	11/22/2019	ELA	88
			03/19/2019	MATH	100
			05/20/2019	SCIENCE	97
FR364701					95
					87.125

While the previous two examples were detailed reports, PROC REPORT also enables the creation of summary reports. The GROUP option in the DEFINE statements tells SAS what variables to group information by. Here, we are grouping to the StudentID, Race, and Gender level. This means the output table will only have one row per unique StudentID, Race, and Gender combination.

The WHERE option specifies that we are only including records without missing scores in the output. The COLUMN statement lists the variables to include in the report and sets up the same headings as the previous example. Notice that the COLUMN statement also includes variable names for computed variables and creates another variable called Score2 that is equivalent to the Score variable. This is necessary because we want to do two different types of analysis with the Score variable in the code below. The DEFINE N statement tells SAS to count the records in each group. Since each student only has one race and one gender, it is counting how many exams each student has taken. While most students have 3 exam scores, we can see in the example above that student "SG547868" is missing a "SCIENCE" Score. Based on the WHERE option excluding missing scores, she will only have a count of 2 for her Exam Count as her missing test score row was excluded.

Since we are reporting one row per student, we need to do some sort of calculation on any additional variables that we include, or the GROUP option will not work. If we used the statement – DEFINE score / DISPLAY 'Exam Score' – for example, all three rows for each student would be printed since we did not tell SAS to compute any calculation on Exam Score. To make sure there is only one row per student, the DEFINE Score statement uses the ANALYSIS mean option, and the DEFINE Score2 statement uses the ANALYSIS max option to report each student's average and maximum exam scores in separate columns labeled Exam Score Average and Exam Score Max in the report.

Next, we DEFINE two additional variables, Extra_Credit and Final_Score and use the COMPUTED option to tell SAS that we are creating these variables in the compute block below. The compute block creates a variable called Extra_Credit and gives each student a value of 2 points. A second compute block creates the variable called Final_Score by taking the mean of each student's exam scores (denoted by Score.mean) and then adding the Extra_Credit variable, or the 2 bonus points, to each student's Score (Table 57).

```
proc report DATA=input.Demo_Exam (WHERE=(Score~=.)) ;
    COLUMN ('Student Exam Scores 2019' ('Student Info'
    StudentID Race Gender) ('Exam Info' N Score Score=Score2
    Extra_Credit Final_Score));
    DEFINE StudentID / GROUP 'Student ID';
    DEFINE Race / GROUP;
    DEFINE Gender / GROUP;
    DEFINE N / 'Exam Count';
    DEFINE Score / ANALYSIS mean 'Exam Score Average';
    DEFINE Score2 / ANALYSIS max 'Exam Score Max';
    DEFINE Extra_Credit / computed 'Extra Credit';
    DEFINE Final_Score / computed 'Final Score';
    COMPUTE Extra_Credit;
        Extra_Credit=2;
    ENDCOMP;
    COMPUTE Final_Score;
        Final_Score= Score.mean+Extra_Credit;
    ENDCOMP;
run;
```

Table 57: PROC REPORT Group Option

Student Exam Scores 2019							
Student Info			Exam Info				
Student ID	Race	Gender	Exam Count	Exam Score Average	Exam Score Max	Extra Credit	Final Score
FR364701	Hispanic	Male	3	95	100	2	97
MU100256	Black	Female	3	90	98	2	92
SG547868	White	Female	2	71	74	2	73

The final example utilizes the ACROSS option to transpose the exam data for each subject. This means that rather than three separate rows listing the exam score for each student in each subject, there will be one row per student that lists each subject as its own column. Now, all three exam scores for the student are in the same row rather than being on three separate rows.

The COLUMN statement creates a spanning header called 'Student Exam Scores 2019'. It then lists the variables to include in the report. Notice that there is a comma after the variable subject, and then Exam_Date and Score are listed. This tells SAS to report the Exam_Date and the Score for each subject the student took an exam in. This means these two columns will appear in the table once for "ELA", again for "MATH", and again for "SCIENCE". Since we are still grouping the data by StudentID, Race, and Gender, we must specify an ANALYSIS option for Exam_Date and exam Score. I chose the default ANALYSIS option for Exam_Date (sum) and mean for exam Score, but I could have chosen anything because the across option for subject specifies that each Exam_Date and Score be written for each subject. Essentially, we are telling SAS to take the sum/mean of a single number, which is simply that same number. Taking the minimum or maximum of a single number also results in the same number, so again, the ANALYSIS option that you choose here does not matter in this specific scenario (Table 58).

```
proc report DATA=input.demo_exam;
    COLUMN ('Student Exam Scores 2019' StudentID Race Gender
    subject, (exam_date score));
    DEFINE StudentID / GROUP 'Student ID';
    DEFINE Race / GROUP;
    DEFINE Gender / GROUP;
    DEFINE subject / across;
    DEFINE exam_date / ANALYSIS 'Exam Date';
    DEFINE score / ANALYSIS mean 'Exam Score';
run;
```

Table 58: PROC REPORT Across Option

			Student Exam Scores 2019					
			Subject					
			ELA		**MATH**		**SCIENCE**	
Student ID	**Race**	**Gender**	**Exam Date**	**Exam Score**	**Exam Date**	**Exam Score**	**Exam Date**	**Exam Score**
FR364701	Hispanic	Male	11/22/2019	88	03/19/2019	100	05/20/2019	97
MU100256	Black	Female	11/22/2019	90	03/19/2019	82	05/20/2019	98
SG547868	White	Female	11/22/2019	74	03/19/2019	68	05/20/2019	.

9.3 Output Delivery System

The Output Delivery System (ODS) allows users to format SAS output into colorful, easy-to-read charts and reports that are more user-friendly than the traditional, default output. It can convert SAS output into other file formats like HTML, RTF, PDF, XLSX, etc. ODS can be used to change things like colors, fonts, borders, headers, and styles for reports and control image size, resolution, style, and file format for charts and graphs.

This functionality is especially useful when you need to reproduce the same report every so often but with updated data. For example, suppose you need to create quarterly PDF reports on your company's earnings. You can use SAS and the ODS functionality to write a program that reads in data, calculates the necessary columns, formats the data in a way that is consistent with your company's style guide, and outputs the calculations into a beautiful PDF. Now, when you need to create the same report for the next quarter of earnings, you can update the program to read in the new input data for the quarter and then rerun the exact same program to generate the report. This saves you time and effort each quarter so that you don't have to copy and paste data into templates (which creates opportunities for errors) or spend hours formatting your output in other software programs.

There are entire books (much longer than this one) that discuss the extensive capabilities of ODS. However, most jobs prefer their reports to be formatted in a customized, specific way. Rather than trying to learn/memorize all of the different ODS functionality, I have found it more helpful to search for specific ODS syntax once I have an idea of what a report needs to look like (e.g., a PDF of a bar chart or a Microsoft Word document with a data table). Once you learn the basics of ODS, there are many SAS resources available to you that can help you create customized reports.

9.3.1 ODS Destinations

ODS takes the data that you specify and puts it into a table or graph template to create one or more output objects. The objects are then sent to specified destinations that are either formatted by SAS (e.g., listing, output) or formatted by third parties (e.g., HTML, RTF, Excel).

Start by telling SAS what destination or file format you want to create the report in. If you wanted to make a PDF, this line would read ODS PDF. Then add the SAS code that you want to run and output the results. Finally, end with an ODS CLOSE statement. In this case, it would be ODS PDF CLOSE. This is called the sandwich method because your SAS code is sandwiched between an ODS statement that opens the file destination and an ODS CLOSE statement that closes the file destination.

```
ODS destination <destination option(s)>;
<SAS code to generate output for destination>;
ODS destination close;
```

If you want to output your results to multiple destinations, you can open several destinations at once and close them individually when you are done or use the ODS _ALL_ CLOSE; statement to close all open destinations at once.

Example syntax for saving charts and graphs to ODS destinations can be found in the ODS Graphics section below.

9.3.2 ODS Graphics

ODS graphics enables you to create interesting visual representations of your data in the form of charts and graphs that you can use in your reports. If you are working in Base SAS® version 9.3 or later, ODS graphics is included and available to use. The most common charts and graphs I work with are histograms, bar charts, line plots, scatter plots, and box plots. These, and many other chart options, are available using the SGPLOT procedure.

```
proc sgplot DATA=input-table <options>;
plot statement(s) / <options>;
<appearance statements>;
run;
```

Let's say we want to examine whether there is any correlation between height and weight. In other words, on average, as height increases, does weight also increase? We can explore this by generating a scatterplot of the Height and Weight data from the Health_Chart data set. The code below tells SAS to read the Health_Chart data set and create a scatter plot with the Weight variable plotted on the Y axis of the chart and the Height variable plotted on the X axis.

```
proc sgplot data=input.health_chart;
scatter y=weight x=height;
run;
```

Figure 15: Scatter Plot Default

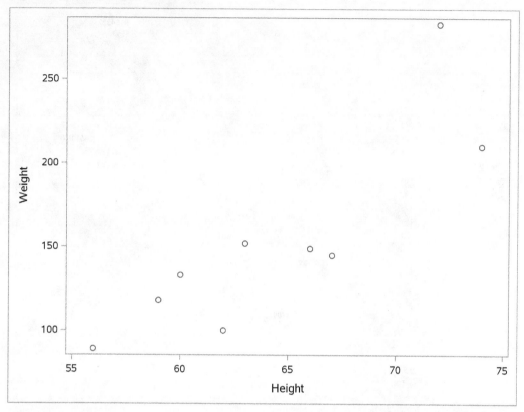

This scatterplot ([Figure 15](#)) indicates that Height and Weight are correlated, though there are a few outliers (or data points that are extremely different from the trend). The doctor might want to follow up with these patients. However, it is impossible to know which patients to follow up with from this scatter plot alone. The doctor might want a customized scatterplot that displays all the information she needs in one place.

The code below updates the scatterplot to include data labels for each point that displays the PatientID. It specifies where the data labels should be printed with the DATALABELPOS option of TOP. This indicates that the label should be printed on top of the data points, though you can specify TOP, BOTTOM, RIGHT, LEFT, or a combination of these positions (e.g., TOPLEFT). Also, to make the points more visible and appealing, we can specify in the MARKERATTRS option that the symbol for each point should be a filled-in diamond, and the SIZE should be increased to 14.

```
proc sgplot data=input.Health_Chart;
scatter y=Weight x=Height / datalabel=Patient_ID
datalabelpos=top
markerattrs=(symbol=DiamondFilled size=14px);
run;
```

Figure 16: Scatter Plot Fancy

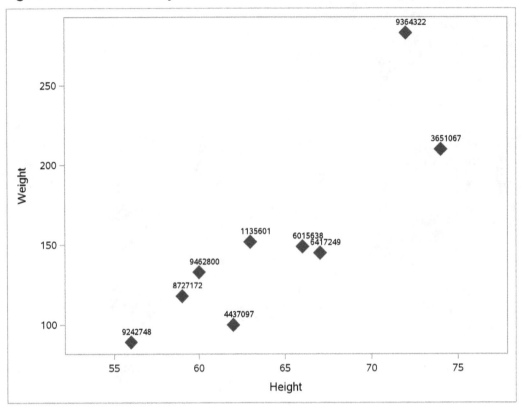

The updated scatterplot (Figure 16) prints each PatientID above each scatterplot point that is now represented by a large, filled-in diamond. The doctor now has the information that is needed to follow up with patients as necessary.

Next, we'd like to create a histogram of the Age reported in the GSS data set to see what the Age distribution was for the respondents. Histograms are like bar charts but for numeric data. There are no spaces between the bars because the width of the bars, or bins, are all the same and represent the distance between categories. This is different from bar charts that represent categorical data. Each bar in a bar chart denotes a discrete category, like Red, Yellow, and Blue, which do not have a measurable distance between them like numeric data does (e.g., the distance between the number 1 and number 3 is 2). We can output our Age histogram to a PDF so that it is easy to email and share with others. The ODS PDF statement opens the PDF destination, and the FILE= statement specifies the location and file name for where the PDF document should be saved. The ODS PDF CLOSE statement tells SAS that we are done outputting information to this destination so that it can be closed and saved.

```
ods pdf file = "&output.\Histogram_Default.pdf";
proc sgplot data=input.GSS;
    histogram Age;
run;
ods pdf close;
```

Figure 17: Histogram Default

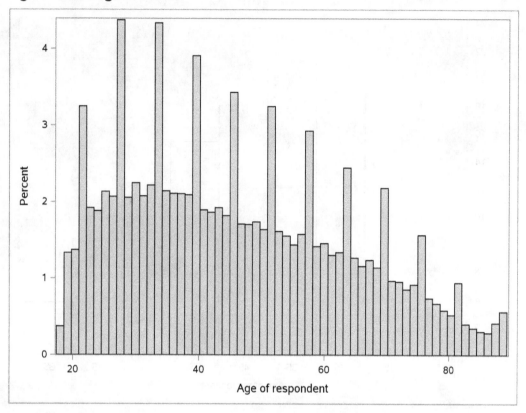

This histogram (Figure 17) displays the Age of the respondents on the X axis (the width of the bar) and the percentage of respondents in each category (the height of the bar) on the Y axis. This histogram is challenging to read. The bars are skinny, and it is difficult to tell what Age range (bin) is represented by each bar. It would be easier to read this histogram if the bars were sectioned into decades.

The code below updates the bar chart to show the midpoint of the bins (SHOWBINS option). It specifies that the first midpoint represented on the X axis should be 5 (BINSTART=5), and the bin width should be 10 (BINWIDTH=10). This creates nine bars representing ages 0-10, 10-20, 20-30, and so on. The midpoint of each bin (e.g., 5, 15, 25) are displayed on the chart as the bin markers. This code also specifies that the Y axis, representing the percentage of respondents in each bin, should start at 0 and go up to 24% with a tick mark for each 2% increase.

```
ods pdf file = "&output.\Histogram_Fancy.pdf";
proc sgplot data=input.GSS;
    histogram Age/ showbins binstart=5 binwidth=10;
    yaxis values=(0 to 24 by 2);
run;
ods pdf close;
```

Figure 18: Histogram Fancy

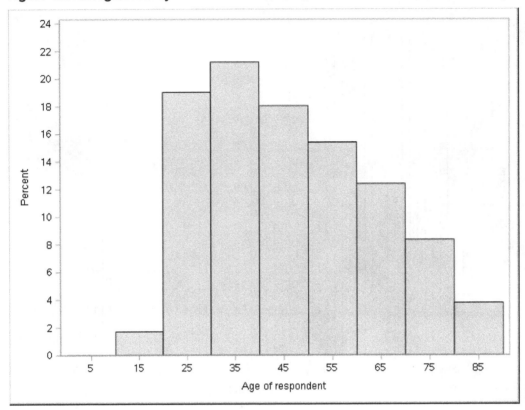

This histogram (Figure 18) is much easier for me to interpret. About 2% of the respondents were between the ages of 10 and 20, while about 21% were between 30 and 40. Much better. Always try to make your life, and the lives of the consumers of your report, easier.

The last example we will look at is a bar chart. Now, each bar represents a category, not a bin. Here, we are creating a Word document (RTF file extension) called BarChart_Default that displays a bar chart of the Marital_Status variable reported in the GSS data. This chart shows each marital status category across the X axis and the number of respondents (frequency count) in each category on the Y axis.

```
ods rtf file = "&output.\BarChart_Default.rtf";
proc sgplot data=input.GSS;
    vbar Marital;
run;
ods rtf close;
```

Figure 19: Bar Chart Default

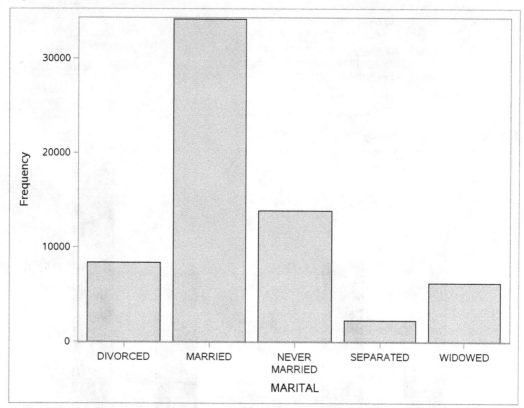

This bar chart (Figure 19) shows that the majority of GSS respondents were married, while the fewest identified as being separated. While this is a solid bar chart, it might raise subsequent questions about each marital status. For example, what is the average Age of the respondents in each category? Are never married individuals typically younger than married people? Are widows typically older? Let's find out.

Here, we modified our bar chart to report the average Age of all respondents in each marital status category on the Y axis. This is done by specifying that the RESPONSE option should equal the Age variable and that the STAT that should be reported is the MEAN for each group. The FILLATTRS option tells SAS that we want our bars to be BLUE, while the DATALABELATTRS option specifies that our data labels should be BLACK with a SIZE of 15 and a BOLD font WEIGHT. The BARWIDTH option must be a value between 0 and 1, with 1 representing the maximum width and 0 representing the narrowest bar possible. The DATASKIN option enables you to add a special effect to your bars. The default value is NONE, but you can try out CRISP, GLOSS, MATTE, PRESSED, and SHEEN to see whether these options make your report more enjoyable to look at. I went with PRESSED here. Finally, I want to label my X and Y axes to clarify what each represents.

```
ods rtf file = "&output.\BarChart_Fancy.rtf";
proc sgplot data=input.GSS;
    vbar Marital/ response=Age stat=mean
    fillattrs=(color=blue)
    datalabelattrs=(color=black size=15 weight=bold)
    barwidth=.5 dataskin=pressed;
    label Age='MEAN AGE' Marital='MARITAL STATUS';
run;
ods rtf close;
```

Figure 20: Bar Chart Fancy

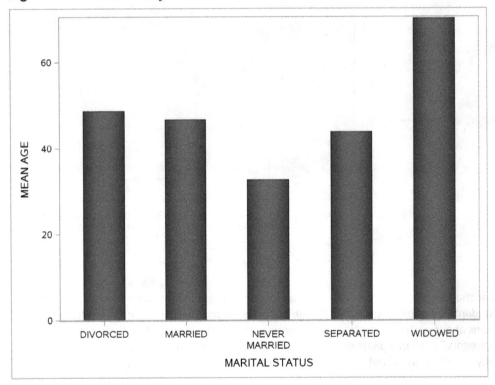

Figure 20 displays the result. For those reading along in an e-book, how are your eyes feeling? That is an intense shade of blue. For those reading along in a printed copy of this book, is that PRESSED effect keeping you awake? There is only so much vividness I can provide in black and white. But it is important to understand that your reports might be viewed in different mediums, so always consider your audience.

We can see from this bar chart that never married individuals do have the lowest mean Age while widowed respondents had the highest Age, on average. There was not much difference in Age between the divorced, married, and separated marital status categories.

10 Introduction to Selected Advanced Topics

Congratulations! If you have made it this far, you can (un)officially call yourself a SAS Novice! Well done. Now you can dive headfirst into the world of analytics with confidence. To help you take that first step from Novice to Noteworthy, here is a brief introduction to two important advanced topics.

10.1 Cloud Analytic Services (CAS)

The emergence of cloud computing has transformed the field of data analytics. Now, computing services (infrastructure, platform, and software) can be delivered over the internet for faster computing time, for less start-up costs (eliminates the need to buy and maintain hardware like servers), and to increase the flexibility to scale up or down easily based on business needs. SAS Viya® and SAS® Cloud Analytic Services (CAS) offer these advantages to users.

SAS Viya® is an open, cloud-enabled platform that supports high-performance analytics. It is a software platform that allows users, businesses, and organizations to access, manage, analyze, and visualize their data all in one place. CAS is a part of the SAS Viya® platform. It is a server that provides a cloud-based run-time environment that utilizes distributed computing for faster run times and high-powered analytics. CAS can use multiple machines or multiple threads on a single machine to speed up processing by designating one controller node and several worker nodes. The controller node splits up the data between the worker nodes, which process data simultaneously and return the results to the controller node to assemble.

While Base SAS® code (the traditional SAS code that has been covered so far in this book) can be run in SAS Viya®, some Base SAS® procedures can be routed through the CAS server, while others must still run through a traditional SAS Compute server. If you are working with large data sets (e.g., more than 25GB) or a step takes a long time to process on the traditional compute server, consider using the CAS server. SAS maintains documentation on what Base SAS® procedures can run CAS actions[13]. Some procedures are not CAS-enabled and must be rewritten in the CAS Language (CASL) to be routed through the CAS server. CASL is a scripting language that is quite

---

[13] Currently located in the SAS® 9.4 and SAS Viya® 3.4 Programming Documentation found at: https://go.documentation.sas.com/doc/en/pgmsascdc/9.4_3.4/proc/p0nnkdmqmz48w8n1kgofzc7mcla4.htm

different from the traditional SAS programming language. To learn more about CASL, see the CASL Programmer's Guide[14].

To run processes through CAS, you must first connect to a CAS server using a CAS statement. Then, tables must be copied from physical locations into memory. Users can set up a caslib where in-memory tables can be loaded and accessed during the CAS session. Calculations are completed in memory, and any resulting tables must be saved back out to a physical location if you want to access them after the CAS session has ended.

10.2 Macro Language

I absolutely hated macros when I first started coding. I am a very linear thinker who loves transparency and seeing exactly what is happening in what order. Marcos can be sneaky, powerful, and nested, which made me feel a bit like I was unpacking a nesting doll without knowing what would be in the center. Because I did not fully understand how they worked, I fought against using them in my code for a long time. I can't believe I am admitting this in writing, but I was wrong. I don't say that often, so macros really are special.

The SAS® macro language can be viewed as a form of shorthand that drastically reduces the amount of code that you need in a program, increasing efficiency and reducing opportunities for error. Macro variables, in their most basic form, are text substitutions. In contrast, macro programs are often referred to as programs that write programs.

SAS recognizes two symbols as macro triggers when they occur at the beginning of a word. The & symbol (e.g., &LIBREF) indicates a macro variable reference, while the % sign (e.g., %LET) indicates a macro statement, function, or call. When SAS encounters a macro trigger as it reads through the code of your program, the macro reference is routed to a component called the macro processor.

The macro processor replaces macro variables with the appropriate text substitutions (that are then sent back to the input stack to be compiled). SAS reads only the substituted text while executing the program. For macro programs, the macro processor compiles the program and saves it. Then, when that macro program is called later in the session, SAS executes the stored macro program code.

10.2.1 Macro Variables

Macro variables store text. You can think of a macro variable as text substitution. Consider some articles that you've read with acronyms. The acronym is defined at the beginning of the paper (e.g., Graphics Interchange Format (GIF)), and then the abbreviation can be used throughout the

---

[14] https://documentation.sas.com/doc/en/pgmsascdc/9.4_3.4/caslpg/titlepage.htm

rest of the article (GIF[15]) to save the writer from having to type out the long definition over and over again. Macro variables function in the same way. You first define the macro variable (which creates an entry in the symbol table). Then, every time you reference that variable, SAS knows to substitute in the definition that you created earlier.

One way to create a macro variable is to use a %LET statement. For example, if you want to create a macro variable called qtr that you populate as Q1, Q2, Q3, or Q4 depending on what quarter you are running the report in, you would use the %LET qtr=Q1; statement when it's the first quarter and the %LET qtr=Q2; in the second quarter, and so on. Now, you can write your program code and use the &qtr macro variable throughout anywhere the quarter is required. The &qtr macro variable will be replaced with the text Q1, Q2, Q3, or Q4 depending on what you have defined qtr as in your %LET statement at the beginning of the program. This is super helpful because you do not have to do a find-and-replace every time you need to update the quarter or create and save 4 separate SAS programs. You just update the definition of qtr in the %LET statement at the beginning of your program to reference the current quarter, and it updates the code throughout the entire program accordingly. No more find and replace. Just update the %LET statement and you are done!

It is important to note that if there is no space after your macro variable reference, you must use a period to denote the end of the macro variable. Without a space or a period, SAS does not recognize where the end of the macro variable reference is and continues to read in extra text. For example, if you have a variable called Q1_earnings in your data set and defined your &qtr macro variable as Q1, you could not call that variable by using &qtr_earnings in your report code. SAS will think the entire variable name is the macro reference, and it will not be able to find &qtr_earnings in the symbol table. If you need to call that variable, you will need to refer to it as &qtr._earnings so that SAS knows to stop reading when it gets to the period and replaces &qtr. with Q1 and therefore writes out the full variable name Q1_earnings.

When you create a macro variable, it is called a user-defined macro. These macro variables are saved in the global symbol table when defined outside of a macro program and apply to all code run during the SAS session. Alternatively, when macro variables are defined inside a macro program, they are saved to a local symbol table that only applies to that macro program. Local definitions are only used inside of a specific macro program, whereas global definitions are applied throughout all of your code.

SAS also has some automatic macro variables[16] that are defined in the global symbol table when SAS starts up. These automatic variables often describe things about your session, like the current date (&SYSDATE), the day of the week (&SYSDAY), and your user ID (&SYSUSERID). These automatic variables can be used throughout your code so that you don't have to constantly

---

[15] I refuse to pronounce this acronym as JIF for the same reason I refuse to acknowledge that a tomato is fruit. No tomato smoothies for me please.
[16] https://go.documentation.sas.com/doc/en/mcrolref/1.0/p14ym6slnzfstzn1t9yp5v31ijis.htm

update your code with the current date every time you run your program. You can view all macro variables and their associated values in the Log using the following command.

```
%put _all_;
```

10.2.2 Macro Programs

Macro programs are more complex than macro variables and start with a %MACRO <name>; statement and end with a %MEND <name>; statement. When you run the code, the macro program is compiled and saved to the macro catalog. Only when that macro program is called with the %NAME statement does the macro program code execute. While macro variables are especially useful when a text reference needs to be updated throughout a program, macro programs are particularly helpful when you need to loop through data multiple times.

For example, if you want to produce a report for each district in a state that reads in the district's data, performs calculations, and outputs the results for each district, it might be helpful to write a macro program. That way, you create the report code only once, but each time you call the macro and input the specific district name and number, the report uses the appropriate information for that district only when generating each report. Rather than having to write a separate program for each district, you write one macro program that writes each district's program for you.

While the specifics of macro programming are outside the scope of this book (you can have macro program calls inside of other macro programs!), I hope this explanation helps you better conceptualize what macros are so that you are not terrified of them like I was and feel confident learning more about them and creating macros of your own.

Appendix A: Resources

Table 59: Resource Links

Resource	Link
CASL Programmer's Guide	https://documentation.sas.com/doc/en/pgmsascdc/9.4_3.4/caslpg/titlepage.htm
Data for Good	https://www.sas.com/en_us/data-for-good.html.
SAS® 9.4 and SAS Viya® 3.5 Programming Documentation	https://go.documentation.sas.com/doc/en/pgmsascdc/9.4_3.5/pgmsaswlcm/home.htm
SAS Automatic Macros	https://go.documentation.sas.com/doc/en/mcrolref/1.0/p14ym6slnzfstzn1t9yp5v31ijis.htm
SAS Colors	https://support.sas.com/content/dam/SAS/support/en/books/pro-template-made-easy-a-guide-for-sas-users/62007_Appendix.pdf
SAS Functions	https://go.documentation.sas.com/doc/en/pgmsascdc/9.4_3.5/lefunctionsref/p1g8bq2v0o11n6n1gpij335fqpph.htm
SAS Library	https://documentation.sas.com/doc/en/pgmsascdc/9.4_3.5/basess/n0a43pssblhvu0n1b51enwlu24n5.htm
SAS Log	https://go.documentation.sas.com/doc/en/pgmsascdc/9.4_3.5/lepg/p119kau8rt2ebgn1bzaipafu6jp3.htm
SAS Procedures that use CAS Actions	https://go.documentation.sas.com/doc/en/pgmsascdc/9.4_3.4/proc/p0nnkdmqmz48w8n1kqofzc7mcla4.htm
SAS® Studio – Free Version	https://welcome.oda.sas.com/
SAS Style Attributes	https://go.documentation.sas.com/doc/en/pgmsascdc/9.4_3.5/odsug/p1pt77toue3iyun0z4l9gth5as9f.htm
SAS Users Group: General	https://www.sas.com/en_us/connect/user-groups.html
SAS Users Group: The Boston Area Resources Page	https://www.basug.org/resources
SAS Video Portal	https://video.sas.com/

Appendix B: Create GSS SAS Data Set

I downloaded the General Social Survey (GSS) data from https://gss.norc.org/get-the-data. I
saved it as a Statistical Package for the Social Sciences (SPSS) file (extension .sav) since .sas7bdat
was not an available option. I imported this file into SAS, kept only the variables of interest,
and reformatted the variables. Several variables of interest were read in as numeric values
with character formats that defined what each number represented (for example, 1=MALE and
2=FEMALE). I created new variables that used the put function to save these character formats as
the actual values for each variable to make working with this data easier for the examples in this
book. The code used to import and format the data is below.

```
%let input = C:\Users\kirby\Desktop\book_data\input_data;
libname input "&input.";
options VALIDVARNAME=V7;
/*GSS Data*/
proc import out=gss_imp
     datafile="&input.\GSS7218_R3.sav"
     dbms=SAV replace;
run;
data gss_imp2;
     set gss_imp;
     keep year id wrkstat marital age degree sex race partyid class;
run;
data gss_imp3;
     set gss_imp2;
     if marital>. then marital2=put(marital, maritala.);
     else marital2="";
     if wrkstat>. then wrkstat2=put(wrkstat, wrkstata.);
     else wrkstat2="";
     if degree>. then degree2=put(degree, degreea.);
     else degree2="";
if sex>. then sex2=put(sex, sexa.);
     else sex2="";
     if race>. then race2=put(race, racea.);
     else race2="";
     if partyid>. then partyid2=put(partyid, partyida.);
     else partyid2="";
```

```
        if class>. then class2=put(class, classa.);
        else class2="";
        drop marital wrkstat degree sex race partyid class;
run;
data "&input.\GSS.sas7bdat";
        set gss_imp3;
        rename marital2=MARITAL wrkstat2=WRKSTAT degree2=DEGREE
        sex2=SEX race2=RACE partyid2=PARTYID class2=CLASS;
run;
```